ANYTHING WRONG WITH BEING A KIND PERSON?

Why Successful People Are Passionate About Charity

Patrick Lim

Table of Contents

COPYRIGHT 5

Chapter One 6

Why Most Successful People Do Charity 6

    What Is Charity? 6

    Charity For Name 7

    Worldly Motivation of Charity 8

    Challenges of Charity 10

    The Real Purpose of Charity 11

    Charity Is Meant For The Spirit 13

    Benefits Of Giving To Charity 13

    Reasons To Donate To Charity 16

Chapter Two 22

Law Of Attraction 22

    What is the Law of Attraction? 24

    What Science says? 26

    How to Use Law of Attraction 29

    A Word Of Caution 31

    Using The Law Of Attraction For Our Purpose 32

    Our Passion 32

    The Whole 33

    Applying The Law Of Attraction 34

    Taking Stock 35

    Tips on How to Use the Law of Attraction to Become Successful 35

Conclusion 37

Chapter Three 40
How A Scammer Always Ends Up With? 40

    How To Spot A Scam 41

    The Importance Of Spotting A 419 Scam 41

    What To Look For In A 419 Scam 44

    Characteristics Of Specific Types Of 419 Scams 51

    The Fraud of Ponzi Schemes 54

    How these scammers and fraudsters always end up 56

Chapter Four 60
Successful People Often Have Great Ambitions And Dreams . 60

    The Ability To Dream 60

    Failures, Don't Let Them Bog You Down 61

    Have Specific Goals And Pursue Them 62

    Choose Wisely 63

    Helping the vulnerable in the society 63

    How committed are you to reach your objective and then based on your burning desire? 66

    How To Be A Leader Shaped Leader To Be A Highly Effective Leader For The Vulnerable Society 70

    The Leader Shaped Leader 70

    Making It Happen: Living The Work, Doing The Story For The Glory! 73

Chapter Five 86
Why Do You Really Need Leadership Skills To Effect Changes? 86

Why is leadership so important today? 86
How To Be More Compassionate As A Leader 90
How to find your passion 92

Chapter Six **98**

What Is A Charity Foundation? **98**

What's a Charity Foundation? 98
Charity Foundations: Good or Bad? 99
Considering Starting Your Own Charity Foundation? 101
The Distinctions Between Private Foundation and Public Charity 105
What is a Public Charity? 105
What is a Private Foundation? 106
Major Examples of Private Foundations and Philanthrophy 107
Public Charities That Act as Foundations 111
How Does a Charity Work? 113

Chapter Seven **116**

Who Says Foundations Can't Make Money? **116**

Different Types Of Foundations 117
Non-Operating Vs. Operating Foundations 118
Private Foundation Rules 120
Benefits Of A Private Foundation Vs. A Public Charity 121
Advantages of Private Foundations over Public Charities ... 123
Benefits of a Private Foundation: 124
How does a charity trust/foundation work allow the rich to keep their money? 130

Chapter Eight **133**

What do you want to leave behind if you leave the world? .133
    Hope to leave a legacy of love?...135
    Hope to leave a legacy of purpose? 136
    Legacy of excellence or inspiration?....................................136
    Legacy of encouragement? 137

Conclusion 144

COPYRIGHT

ANYTHING WRONG WITH BEING A KIND PERSON?

Copyright © 2020 by Patrick Lim.

Edited and typeset by Ade Abdul.

All rights reserved. No part of this book may be reproduced, stored in a retrieval system, or transmitted in any form or by any means, electronic, mechanical, photocopying, recording, scanning, or otherwise, without the prior written permission of the publisher.

ASIN: B087ZV5YN9 (Digital Edition)

ISBN: 9798642981191 (Paperback)

Any references to historical events, real people, or real places are used fictitiously. Names, characters, and places are products of the author's imagination.

Published by Kindle Direct Publishing, in the United States of America.

First printing edition May 4, 2020.

Printed by Amazon.com Services LLC,

Monee, IL, USA

Chapter One

Why Most Successful People Do Charity

Years ago I made it my desire to be successful in life and be able to give back to the world. I was raised on the principle that you should leave the world a better place than when you came. I have searched high and low, read books, magazines, websites, listened to podcasts, and watched videos seeking guidance in my goals to be, in the words of Borat, a 'Great Success.'

Although the idea of success is different to every person whether it be money, fame, or something as simple as to have a good family life. I have learned that the rules and advice to reach your idea of success and giving back are the same everywhere and over time.

I have been able to make a list of the most common advice that I have collected from those who have made it and I would be starting with charity.

What Is Charity?

Charity is one of the greatest virtues of mankind. Every religion asks its followers to engage in charities for the fellow human beings and even to other living beings. Charity means using your energy, talent, resources, money, possessions, or whatever else, to help people who need them.

Jesus Christ asked his followers to do good to the people who are less privileged in the society.

'But when you give a banquet, invite the poor, the crippled, the lame, the blind, and you will be blessed. Although they cannot repay you, you will be repaid at the resurrection of the righteous.' (Luke 14:13-14).

The Holy Quran as well compels Muslims to perform charity to attain the love of God and follow the path of righteous in the following words: *'You cannot attain to righteousness unless you spend (in charity) out of what you love.'* (The Holy Quran 3:92)

The basic spirit behind the charity in religion is that man must share what God has given to him. Thus, charity is also a means of giving justice to the fellow human beings and to serve God as all people are the children of God.

Yet, charity must not be done for getting any benefit in return from this world in any form because then it become business and trading of one type of material possession (wealth, time, knowledge etc.) with other type of material possession (name, fame, respect from society etc).

It has to be done without any expectation as God Himself rewards those who do charity.

An ideal act of charity is similar to throwing your money into the river, which is done silently and without any expectation or even a possibility of return.

Charity For Name

Though charity is a great virtue in religions, yet it is often practiced by worldly and material people who do not have much religion affiliation. Charity is done by people who may not have any believe in heaven or God. Bill Gates, who after being the richest man in the world for fourteen years, decided to quit from his company Microsoft, to work full time for the charitable activity of his foundation viz. Bill & Melinda Gates Foundation. Bill Gates is not alone in such charitable works.

Warren Buffet, the second richest man in the world too plans to donate the more than $37 billion from his $44 billion fortune to the Bill and Melinda Gates Foundation. Almost all the biggest charities of the world are set up by some of the richest man of the world, who donated most of their fortune for the charitable work.

Most of these people are not known to be religious and even spiritual. Yet they were motivated by their inherent desire to do good for all human beings or to fulfill the desire of God. *What motivates even a non-religious person to do charity, if they have no faith in God or rewards after this life?*

Worldly Motivation of Charity

Most people become charitable once the money stop giving them satisfaction. This can be explained from the following example:

Suppose you are stranded in a desert and thirsty for days. You are about to die if you do not get water in a few moments. A person approaches you with a glass of water and asks $1000 as the price of one glass of water. You argue with him saying that the price is too high. He says that if you want it, this is the price you have to pay. You pay the price reluctantly as you need the water desperately.

However, once you have drunk your first glass of water, he offers you the next glass of water at the same price. You will refuse to pay as your desperation has reduced. May be you can still pay $100 for one glass of water. Thus the value of water would continue to diminish with every glass you drink. Soon a time would come, when you will refuse to drink a glass of water, even if the person pays you $1000.

The value of money too reduces for every person and gradually becomes a liability rather than an asset as excess money brings with it many problems and miseries in life. A rich person suffers from the threat of life as many people would like to snatch his money. He loses respect and love of the common man who feels jealous and even angry of his riches and his lifestyle, which they cannot afford. They often brand him capricious, dishonest and even thief of the society.

Thus excess wealth instead of giving any satisfaction becomes a source of pain to the rich man. The excess money is like excess weight of the body, which instead of making you beautiful, makes you ugly; instead of making you healthy, makes you unhealthy and instead of making you happy, makes you unhappy.

How many people would mind losing weight, if it would have been possible to give your excess weight to a person without any pain? Can there be any sacrifice involved in giving your excess weight, which you do not want anyway? *That is why Koran said that you must give what you love and not what you dislike.*

Yet most people continue to attach themselves with the excess wealth or weight, as it is extremely painful to part away something that has become part of you. The wise men, however, decide to shed their excess wealth to gain what they lost in the process of acquiring wealth. They donate their wealth and their time in charitable work so that they can gain respect from the society.

In a way, this may not be a charity but the maximization of the worldly pleasure that comes from compliments and respects by spending some money in the name of charity.

Challenges of Charity

It is easy to throw your money in the name of charity, but extremely difficult to do charity that does good to the world. Donations, if given to the wrong person, may instead of doing any good for the society may do considerable harm to the world. Nowadays, thousands of charities have cropped up merely to receive donations from such people who have lost the pleasure of money in the name of charity.

The right type of charity is explained in Gita in following words. Lord Krishna says *'Charity that is given as a matter of duty, to a deserving candidate who does nothing in return, at the right place and time, is called a Saattvika or True charity.'*(Gita 17:20)

Therefore, all charities have to be given to a deserving person at the right place and time. If the rich person is only interested in his interest viz. getting publicity and worldly name and fame, he may be least bothered to the use of charity. As a result, the charity often goes in the hands of the unscrupulous people as they are more likely to convince the rich persons for the share of his charity than a deserving person who may be too dignified to seek alms from a rich person.

Thus the charity given for the purpose of achieving name and fame from the world often results into failure as the world in severe in criticism, if the charity is distributed to wrong people. Thus the person, whose purpose of charity was to get worldly returns, often feel disappointed as his investment in the form of charity fail to produce the desired results.

Jesus, therefore, asks the people to do the charity without publicity and expectation as God rewards those who do not seek any fruits in this world.

'Be careful not to do your 'acts of righteousness' before men, to be seen by them. If you do, you will have no reward from your Father in heaven. So when you give to the needy, do not announce it with trumpets, as the hypocrites do in the synagogues and on the streets, to be honored by men. I tell you the truth, they have received their reward in full.

But when you give to the needy, do not let your left hand know what your right hand is doing, so that your giving may be in secret. Then your Father, who sees what is done in secret, will reward you. (Matthew 6:1-4)

The Holy Koran too emphasizes that the spirit of charity more important then the act of charity. It gives benefit only if one gives it voluntarily out of love of God or humanity rather than a duty that is forced upon them by scriptures. Charity can not be measured in terms of dollars, but measured in terms of the spirit of the giver as Koran says, *'A kind word with forgiveness is better than charity followed by injury.. . . O you who believe, make not your charity worthless by reproach and injury, like him who spends his wealth to be seen by people. . .'* (2:263-264)

The Real Purpose of Charity

Charity in reality is a test of the belief of God. It hardly changes the world or the people to whom the charity is given. However, it transforms the person who gives charity. It is easy to say that one love God and his children, but few people can follow up their words in deeds. Charity without expectation of return in possible only when a person truly believes in God or the Spirit. It is not easy to give away the worldly things to someone without any expectation of returns.

Every act of charity establishes that the charitable man has been able to develop detachment from the worldly possessions including fame and name, which is possible only if the person, is really spiritually awakened. Yet, nothing goes waste in this world. It only transforms into another form by the laws of nature. The material things, therefore, get converted into spiritual realization by the act of charity.

The principles of Karma as enshrined in Gita, states that every action is like a seed that automatically results into the fruit as per the laws of nature. *Whatever you sow, so will you reap* is an old proverb. The world seems to work on this basic principle of action and reaction.

Thus whenever, a person performs any act, he gets something material in return. If we do our job in the office, we are paid our salaries. When you put some money in bank you get interest. When you invest in shares, your investment increases or decreases with the share market.

All actions results into some results. Charity is no exception. All acts of charities are highly rewarded by this world. The world, tries to return what you have given to it. However, if you don't accept the return in terms of money, it tries to honor you by words of praise. If you even refuse praise and honor, it respects you from the bottom of the heart.

Every piece of wealth, if sacrificed in this world, results into some worldly returns in this world itself. The nature tries to balance your acts in a way that the world does not feel obliged by you. It pays all material charity with material rewards. All material rewards, however, binds the man to the world and such acts of kindness can not be said to be unselfish. The people receiving the charity feel inferior to the people who give charity.

The glorification of charity in this world, therefore, does not provide any spiritual satisfaction to the person as the charity does not remain charity after being paid by the world in kind or by an alternative coin.

Charity Is Meant For The Spirit

One need not to wait for the afterlife to get the real benefits of charity because charity provides instant benefits. However, the benefits are not material but spiritual which satisfies the soul of the person and brings happiness and peace in his life. Only by charity one can feel the divine happiness in his soul which comes by giving the material possession of the self to other fellow beings without expectation.

Since the receiver can't pay back the material wealth, his blessings and best wishes brings joys to the giver. The result is much more contented life for the giver as he has been able to at least partially repay the debt of the world and that of God.

Benefits Of Giving To Charity

Charity giving has many benefits. These include the obvious, stated benefit of the Charity's purpose, as well as personal benefits. A more familiar personal benefit may be fulfilling a belief in a cause. This may include helping someone physically, financially, or emotionally. There are also additional personal benefits, including enhanced stability both emotional and mental. Giving to charity makes you a healthier person.

Beyond these intellectually credible benefits, charity has a mystical quality that is more than the sum of its parts. This can be appreciated when brightened by the light and life of the soul. To illustrate, people regularly give charity in someone's honor, and even more - they give charity to a cause so that someone they know should merit help in what they need.

When 'A' gives charity to 'B' that 'C' should be helped, is in the realm of the mystical. Additionally, this benefit accrues to the giver as well, even (or perhaps all the more so) when the only focus is to help the next person.

The reason being, that the energy we usually put into each good deed we do is limited. Whether it's taking out the garbage, telling someone how nice they look, studying hard, or praying, the amount of energy we invest in it, while possibly great, is not endless.

Charity, on the other hand, enjoys great merit because it embodies the giver's total effort. It takes everything you've got, physical and mental, to earn the money you're giving to charity. Any part of money earned which is then given to charity, contains all that energy. Moreover, even a small amount of charity can save a person's life if the poor person was about to expire God forbid, or it can sustain his life for a certain amount of time. This is why Charity (Tzedaka) actually adds life to the giver. This is because God rewards measure for measure. Just like you added life to the poor person, God adds to your life.

Once upon a time many years ago in Israel, two students of Rabbi Chanina went to the woods to chop wood for the study hall (Beth Hamidrash). A famous astrologer noticed them from a distance and said to the people around him: 'Those two young men will not return alive from the forest.'

The two students were not aware of the awful prediction, and continued their happy conversation. On the edge of town a starving beggar pleaded with them for food. Though the students had only one piece of bread for both of them until they got back, they did share it with the beggar and continued into the forest.

On their return from the forest, some of the original crowd noticed the two young men and began to mock the stargazer. 'Look! Two dead men walking!' 'Maybe you need some Starglasses!'

'No, I insist these people were not destined to live. Somehow they cheated death.' The astrologer called them over and looked into their bundles. There was a terribly poisonous snake, half in one bundle and half in another! He then asked the boys to tell what happened to them that day. They had nothing out of the ordinary to tell, except the story with the beggar.

'Do you see, my friends?' explained the astrologer. 'You can make peace with God by giving a piece of bread to a poor person and saving his life!' 'This act of Charity can save your life!' Some of the people took this advice to heart, giving Charity every day, and everybody lived happily ever after.

Actually, 'Charity' doesn't fully describe what happens when you give a donation to a good cause as God not only creates the world, He conducts and guides it, and everything in it. When someone has the ability to give charity, it is intentional on God's part. We are really therefore, God's trustees. He looks to see us treat our charity giving in a judicious, even merciful manner. Rather than giving out of the goodness of our heart, it's more an act of justice, tempered with mercy.

So you see, charity enables us to generously share life. God then extends our life so we can have the reward of giving more charity.

The benefit of giving charity is more life, so we can give more charity!

Reasons To Donate To Charity

The saying that charity can begin at home is true when we consider the role of charity gifts, and with such a wide variety of charities available to donate to, it's no wonder that some people can feel a little overwhelmed when they first go looking for a charity gift that matches their expectations.

Underlisted here are some of the reasons why it is advised to donate/give to charity:

- **Making The World A Better Place:**

If you've ever been offered help or support without being asked to be paid back in the future, or if you've ever been in a position of being able to help someone that has fallen on hard times, you'll know that these actions are done out of the goodness of one's own heart. These selfless acts are in part what makes human nature truly special.

- **Experience More Pleasure:**

In research conducted by the National Institutes of Health, participants who chose to donate a portion of $100 they were provided enjoyed activated pleasure centers in the brain. Although this experiment was controlled and scientific, it did show that donating money simply makes you feel better, which is something we can all benefit from.

- **Help Others in Need:**

We don't live in a perfect world, and there's never going to be a perfect time to give as there are always people out there in need of help. Whether interest rates are rising, the economy is in the doldrums, or even if you're experiencing financial difficulties of your own, the reality is that when you donate your money, you help others who need it.

- **Get a Tax Deduction:**

If you give to an IRS-approved charity, you can write off donations on your tax return. Certain restrictions do apply, though. Donating your cash is a great way to reduce the amount of money you send off to Uncle Sam, and for a good cause, to boot.

If you're itemizing your tax return, you can report the dollars you contributed to charity for a deduction in your taxable income. Even if you're short on cash, you can donate unwanted items to charity (such as clothing, furniture, and vehicles) and claim the value of these goods as a deduction.

For instance, if you make $70,000 annually and contribute $7,000 (or the equivalent in unwanted items) to charity, then your taxable income is reduced to $63,000 on an itemized return. This can add up to a substantial savings, especially if you're in one of the higher tax brackets.

- **Bring More Meaning to Your Life:**

When you donate money to charity, you create opportunities to meet new people who believe in the same causes that inspire you. That, and making a real impact on those causes, can infuse your everyday life with more meaning. If you've been stuck in a rut, whether personally or professionally, sometimes the simple act of donating cash can do the trick and reinvigorate your life.

- **Promote Generosity in Your Children:**

When your kids see you donating money, they're much more likely to adopt a giving mindset as they grow up. I write from personal experience. I've donated money to a variety of charities over the years and have always made sure to inform my eight-year-old son of my efforts.

Last Christmas, when he and I were shopping at a mall, he spotted a kiosk for a charity and rather than spending some of his allotted money on Christmas gifts, he asked if we could sponsor a hungry child overseas. We signed up then and there. Do the same with your kids and you might see similar results.

- **Motivate Friends and Family:**

When you let your friends and family know of your charitable donations, they may find themselves more motivated to undertake their own efforts to give. It takes a village to address issues such as world poverty, scientific advancement, and early childhood education. Stoking passions in the folks around you is a very positive and tangible effect of your own giving.

- **Realize that Every Little Bit Helps:**

You don't need $10,000 to make a difference in someone's life. In developing countries, even just a few U.S. dollars could result in a week's worth of meals for a starving child, much-needed medical attention, and even improved schooling. Don't just think of your cash donation from an American economic perspective. Often that money can go a lot further elsewhere in the world.

- **Improve Personal Money Management:**

If you set a scheduled $100 donation each month for a particular charity, that can motivate you to be more attentive to your own finances in an effort to ensure you don't default or fall behind in your monthly donations. Anything that gets you to pay closer attention to your bank account is a good thing; especially when it helps those in need.

- **Give, If You Can't Volunteer:**

This might not necessarily be a positive effect of charitable giving, but if you're too busy to volunteer or otherwise donate your time, giving money is the perfect workaround. Never think that you can't improve someone's life or the world itself if your personal or professional schedule won't allow the time. Writing out a check is a simple way to show you're willing to help others in any way you can.

- **Increase Your Community Standing:**

Generous givers tend to have more influence with their pet projects than others do. For instance, one of the organizations I contract with is far more likely to have generous givers serve on the board than people who aren't financially invested in the cause. In turn, these board members are in a better position to influence the agency's decision-making because they have demonstrated their interest and investment time and time again.

The more you give to an organization, the more likely you are to influence that organization's activities.

- **Improves Your Employee Morale:**

Corporate enterprises give for all kinds of reasons, including an improved public image, increased profits, and tax breaks. And, according to research, individual employees who contribute their time or money to a corporate cause are more likely to report improved worker morale.

Participating in your company's giving campaigns can make you feel like a part of your corporate team. Employers who want to improve retention and team-building should offer company giving campaigns and volunteer opportunities for employees.

- **Protects Your Local Community:**

National safety net programs, such as Food Stamps and disability benefits, can be of great benefit to Americans, but giving to community organizations can provide important local safety nets that guarantee vital assistance during crises and emergencies as well. Community organizations tend to respond faster and more appropriately to the needs of local communities than larger organizations do, and these agencies obtain most of their funding from private donations.

Local giving, therefore, provides support for the programs that enhance community well-being.

You might not think that what you give can make a difference but you must think of the butterfly effect. One small change can affect millions or billions of people. The amount you give does not have to be a large sum, but it does have to be given freely. There are many charities that are in dire need of funds to keep their organizations operational. Each small amount adds up.

As the current economy has faltered, the government has received less money from taxes. With government resources stretched, there is little remaining to pay for charitable causes. It is therefore vital that you support the charities that you want in whichever way possible.

One of the most popular charities that people donate to is *Save The Children*. They have many different venues in which they provide funds to places and people that need it. A few other charities to donate to that you might consider are Peta, or many cancer foundations. These are considered some of the best charities to donate to as they are efficient with the funds that people provide them. They do not waste a lot of money on overhead or salaries. The bulk of the funds are spent where it is needed.

Another reason to donate to a charity is that you can see the effects that the charities do in various communities around the world and the nation. They make the world a much better place to live in. Positive changes in one area often spread elsewhere.

Studies have shown that people who do for others are happier. You can affect changes in your local community or globally, the choice is yours. It does not have to be a large amount of money, any amount you decide to donate will be appreciated.

The government can no longer support as much as in the past due to lack of economic resources and helping others will give you a brighter outlook on the world as well as improve your happiness.

The next time you need to buy a present, consider a charity gift through one of the online charity websites.

Chapter Two

Law Of Attraction

"Reality is a projection of your thoughts or the things you habitually think about." — Stephen Richards

All it takes is that increased sense that everything and anything is possible. The Law of Attraction is a compelling theory that appeals instantly to many people and is the idea that the key to drawing something toward you lies with the pull of magnetic attraction.

Consider for a moment what you could achieve if you knew the secret of directing this magnetic pull to bring you the things in life you most desire. The Law of Attraction is an age old concept, which has floated around at the back of the human consciousness for many centuries and The Secret is a bestselling book which revives this idea and brings it up to date.

Many people believe that the fundamental idea of the Law of Attraction comes from Hinduism, and there is also a direct link to this theory in the 1902 book As a Man Thinketh by James Allen, the title of which originates from a Bible verse that states *"As a man thinketh in his heart, so is he."*

For Allen the heart represented the sum repository of a person's desires, dreams and life goals, which could be achieved by attracting all the things that are wanted or needed.

The author of The Secret, Rhonda Byrne, was inspired by another prominent writer Wallace D Wattles, who penned a very popular book in 1910 called The Science of Getting Rich. Wattles had previously experienced a life of failure after failure until he began to apply the power of magnetic pull, and as he imagined himself as a successful writer and a man in control of his own achievements, so the realization of his visions began to come true.

The Law of Attraction is among the most ancient universal laws. It just means to depict that whatever circumstances we face in our life are the result of what we thought in our past. Thoughts dominate our mind; they have to manifest in our life. The circumstances we face, the people we meet, the relationships we make, the money we make, the house we live in; these all are the outcome of what we have been thinking with little bit more concentration or simply saying what we have been thinking the most.

Have you ever observed when you get angry or frustrated in the morning, it often happens that your whole day sucks. The *"whole day sucks"* is a phenomenon that is happening because we attracted it in the morning.

What is the Law of Attraction?

The law of attraction is a belief or theory, that *"like attracts like"*, and that by focusing on positive or negative thoughts, one can bring about positive or negative results. The simple concept of the Law of Attraction has been called many things over the years such as Ask, Believe and Receive, Positive Thinking, New Thought, Science of the Mind and Prosperity Thinking, but it is all based on one idea that flows through the human subconscious, that is you can attract what you most desire or need as long as you practice the correct approach.

First of all you have to understand your true desires, dreams and life goals, and what it is you want or need to achieve them. This is rather like making a cake. You cannot begin until you have assembled all of the right ingredients and equipment, and you have to understand what things you need to get exactly the kind of cake you want, and then once you have everything the power lays in your hands to make a truly marvellous treat. Although this is a simplistic view it does illustrate just how important it is to know your own desires before you can attract what will truly fulfil you.

Speaking shortly I will define the law of attraction in one line: *"What we think, we manifest"*.

It's simple. We attract in our daily life with our thoughts and feelings. For example, if we keep thinking that we have no money in our bank account, we will be attracting *"no money"* in our life. Similarly if we feel like depressed due to workload or other anxieties, we will be welcoming more *"depression and anxieties"*. So we are using this universal law all the time whether we know it or not. Things happening in our daily life are due to this law of attraction.

Simply being ambitious can be a major factor in career success. In a study of 990 people, it was the 'very ambitious' people who were more likely to have been promoted at work, and even more importantly for you lot, the average age of the 'promoted' group was more than four years younger than the group who weren't promoted. This gave us the conclusion that: high ambition = better chance of career success.

"I strongly believe without an ambition, none can be successful," said Ivan Beckley, co-founder of Limitless, a new organisation to raise the ambition of school-aged children in London. *"Ambition is the driving force that says I want to achieve something and I'm going to work towards doing do. Imagine the impact if all our kids had that grasp of true ambition. I can bet you we wouldn't have to force a single child to go to school."*

What Science says?

Thomas Troward, who was among the big guns of the New Thought Movement, claimed that: *"Thought precedes physical form and that "the action of Mind plants that nucleus which, if allowed to grow undisturbed, will eventually attract to itself all the conditions necessary for its manifestation in outward visible form."*

Later on metaphysicians also supported the existence of the law of attraction in our daily life. After that the arrival of the book "The Secret" brought up a great revolution in the societies and religious beliefs. So The Law of Attraction is much more the game of your mind set. If you are sincerely able to abide by the principals of the law, you will discover that you can get anything in your life that you love to achieve.

Law of Attraction is a natural law of nature which attracts into your life whatever you give your attention, energy and focus to.

Let me give you a couple of examples:

There is a person we all have met in our lives which I will call Negative Nellie. Nellie is always complaining about something, generally doesn't feel well and seems to have various aches or pains. She is usually faced with one dilemma after another.

Another individual is one I call Positive Patty. She is a person who seems to always be on a roll. She is always upbeat, seems to enjoy one great event after another, wins things and basically seems to live a charmed life.

Both of these are examples of the Law of Attraction in action. Whatever we give our attention, energy and focus to is attracted into our lives. If we have positive, upbeat thoughts, we will attract positive events into our life. If, on the other hand, we spend our time thinking about negative issues such as debt, lack of free time, unhappy relationships, we are inviting more of the same.

You can learn how to change your life and attract more of what you want into your life and less of what you don't. Basically, change your thoughts and change your life.

I use Law of Attraction every day. It has brought me much more joy and happiness as well as a lot of wonderful things.

Just this past November, my wife and I were in Nevada on business. Our business concluded earlier than expected and we were faced with finding a hotel in the Las Vegas area since that was the airport we were to fly out of. It so happened that there were events going on and available rooms were way out of our price range. I put the Law of Attraction to work while my wife and I decided to take a two day trip to the Grand Canyon and to see friends in Arizona. It was during this trip that my wife found a wonderful deal for us in Las Vegas while checking online. The Luxor, a hotel/casino on the strip in Las Vegas was offering four nights for the price of three. This would work for our budget. She also found availability at a new casino/hotel near the Hoover Dam for the other night we would require and since we both wanted to see the Hoover Dam, this was perfect.

Now, some of you may call it coincidence or just plain luck. For me, I know it was the universes reply to my request. I experience many things like this. This past summer, while traveling back from Arkansas, my wife had me call ahead to a Marriott in Tennessee. I wanted to stay on the river with a room that had a nice view. I called the hotel and requested a room. They made my reservation and when we arrived, found out that we had been upgraded - at no additional charge - to a room on the concierge floor. When we entered our room, we had the most fantastic view plus all the amenities and convenience of the concierge floor! Again, Law of Attraction had brought me more of what I wanted in my life. My wife gets to enjoy the benefits as well.

Most possibly the best example came during the Christmas holidays. My wife and I were scheduled to fly to Colorado Christmas Eve to surprise our grandchildren on Christmas morning. However, all parking lots including the remote were full and people were being asked to have someone drive them to the airport. Having no one available to do this for us (all were away themselves) we had no alternative but to drive ourselves. My wife was planning to drive to her office and take a cab from there. I, on the other hand decided to send my request for a parking space to the universe on the 22nd. On our way to my wife's office on the 24th, we took a chance and drove by the parking lots at the airport.

All were closed but one had an attendant at the gate. We pulled up and I got out and asked if there was any parking open. She told me the airport had just started to allow travellers to use the hourly parking lot at the daily rate! We went directly there and instead of having to take a shuttle from a remote lot to the terminal, we were parked in the covered lot right next to our terminal. Wow! If that wasn't enough, on our return we were 45 minutes late leaving Colorado which meant we would most likely miss our connecting flight in Phoenix. The entire flight I kept seeing us making our flight. When we arrived in Phoenix and ran to our gate at the opposite end of the terminal, the door was already closed. We went to the person at the desk and showed our passes. They called the plane and we were allowed to board! Not only did we make it back home, but our luggage managed to be there waiting for us as well.

I could go on and on, but you get the idea. Since discovering the Law of Attraction, my life has changed dramatically.

How to Use Law of Attraction

As I told you earlier that "What we think, we manifest". What we are going to keep in our mind and concentrate on it, we are actually bringing it in the process of manifestation. Using law of attraction is very easy if you keep a firm belief on your thoughts and visualization.

Here I will teach you how you can use the law of attraction in your life to get anything you desire to achieve. It consists of only three steps:

- Ask
- Feel
- Give

- **Ask:**

The first step is desire what you want in your life. Definitely you cannot get money if you have not planned to get it. Similarly you will not go for vacation in Spain until you have not planned it. So asking is the first step towards using law of attraction in your life.

Sit down, take a pen and paper, relax and think what you desire in your life. Write down everything that comes into your mind whether it's lot of money, a good life partner or whatever; just note it on the paper. Once you have prepared the list of your dreams (wishes), proceed to the next step that is 'feel'.

- **Feel:**

Once you have prepared a list of all of your desires, you have instructed your mind to get ready to achieve. Now start feeling like you have everything in your life that is on that piece of paper (your desires note) and already be grateful for it. If you wrote that you want a lot of money then from now onwards, start feeling like you have lot of money in your account.

Bring up that joy in you when you have $100000 in your account. Feel like you have a perfect partner in your life, and you are living a prosperous life. So start imagining that you have access of everything that you have written on that piece of paper and feel gratitude for this abundance.

What happens here that the universe begins to listen to these consistent thoughts and the manifestation process comes into being. So the main theme of this step is:

"What you want to achieve in your life, feel like you already have it'.

- **Give:**

The last step in the completion of the law of attraction is "to give". There is a principle in this whole process that states:

"The more you give, the more you get back". So give from whatever you have in your life. If you can give happiness to someone, go ahead. If you have money, give it without worrying about the amount. Many people get stuck on this step and have some doubts in their minds, and they are right at it.

As a common person we think that dividing something reduces it. But it is opposite in the law of attraction. This law states that if you give something to someone, you shall get it back multiplied.

The question is "How is it possible?" The answer is quite simple and logical. During the give process, you think like you have a lot of something say its money, and you give some money to others. This feeling of abundance ignites the second process that is 'Feel'. So when giving, feel like you already have abundance of it, and you shall have abundance of it. So 'give' process helps in firming your belief that you already have abundance of everything.

This is so Easy!!

This is what law of attraction states. Ask, feel and give. So the crux of this law lies in your thoughts. Negative thoughts will bring up negative circumstances and vice versa. So start using the law of attraction in your life from now onwards. In the beginning it will take some time to control your thoughts and keep them positive but gradually you will start to have grip over your thoughts and things will start working as the law of attraction will come into action.

It's you who can change your life right now and forever. So go ahead and take advantage of this law and be happy.

A Word Of Caution

A short word about practicing the laws of attraction; don't waste your time dreaming of becoming filthy rich, highly successful and powerful, as though the instructions were contained in some get rich quick manual that you only had to follow to the letter to get what you want, without rhyme or reason of why you should be getting these things. Getting filthy rich is highly unlikely anyway and it is not the purpose of the laws of attraction.

If you study the concept in earnest, begin to practice it with true conviction, you will come to realize that material wealth is less important when the universe begins to endow you with the real riches it possesses.

That isn't to say money cannot be manifested, it can but only in order to achieve a purpose!

Using The Law Of Attraction For Our Purpose

You know, we are each given a purpose to carry out before we land here on earth and moving away from that purpose will only result in difficulties and disillusionment because we are not creating that which was decided for us (by us). It's like swimming against the tide! Did you ever feel there was something you should be doing, that you were missing out on something in your life? Do you sometimes ponder your existence and wonder what the meaning of YOUR life is?

The laws of attraction are set in place to help us on our journey of discovery, it's important to be aware of and in tune with the opportunities around us, to have a clear idea of what it is we want to do and what we want to achieve. After all, you can't buy a train ticket without knowing where you are heading!

Our Passion

The laws of attraction will not work the way we want them to until we have figured out what our real passion is. We each need to discover what it is that makes our heart warm, doing something that makes us feel alive, something which feels natural and as though we were made to do this thing.

This is our passion! When we find our passion and incorporate it into our life, suddenly the cogs of our universe will begin to turn and advance us because we are truly on the right path.

Life will become easier; doors will open, and synchronicity will provide the way forward for us. For me, just whilst writing this short article I have received three emails about the Laws of Attraction, the TV is on (I work at home and the kids are home) and have just heard a commercial that voiced the word passion really loudly about seven times!! You see I am doing what I love ' writing, communicating.

I'm exploring my passion and the universe; or God is nudging and winking at me telling me I am on the right path. Try it out for yourself 'it really does work'.

The Whole

Our passion is there to work for the good of the whole and not only for ourselves, that is how the universe manifests, and this is our place in it. It may not seem obvious that doing something we are passionate about will benefit the world - but in the long view it does, it isn't a selfish act!

That's why we are given our individuality; we are here to work separately as pieces of a jigsaw in order to create the whole picture and our blessings for doing this is real happiness.

Applying The Law Of Attraction

Doing what truly makes us happy people is how we will attract more happiness into our lives and less trouble, strife and illness. Scientists are already proving that our DNA reacts according to our emotions and thus when feelings of gratitude, love and appreciation are felt our DNA becomes fully switched on including our ability to resist disease.

However, When the researchers felt anger, fear, frustration, or stress, the DNA responded by tightening up. It became shorter and SWITCHED OFF many of our DNA codes!

The most extraordinary fact about these tests is that the DNA responded in samples taken out of the body at exactly the same moment and with the exact same reaction as the DNA within the donors' body - and the scientists stopped testing after the Donors and the DNA samples were 50 Miles apart!! Now that's got to be food for thought for those scientists, suggesting there has to be an unseen web of energy that connects the physical to the nonphysical elements of not only our makeup, but our world, where distance as we know becomes redundant regarding these connections!

The idea that we are intrinsically connected both to our earth and the universe around us has always been the major point of the Laws of Attraction, and it seems even science is at last catching up with this knowledge.

The Laws of Attraction may sound simple but actually practicing them is not so easy. The art of focusing one's mind and emotions on positive things, on what we want rather than what we don't want has to be well rehearsed before it can be done without effort.

We can all too easily fall back into complaining mode, focusing on the negative around us and therefore attracting more of it into our lives!

Taking Stock

So this said; the first thing we need to do is to take stock of our life. This is vital if we are to continue to move forward, even if we think we have it all figured out. Sometimes things change; we start to lose hold of the reigns and slip off course because of the many distractions and events that can preoccupy us. Regular contact with our inner mind is essential to keep in check our aims and ambitions, to tap into our purer thoughts and the unconditional love we should be feeling and giving out.

Discarding bad habits and excess baggage that we have collected on the way is good housekeeping and helps us to work WITH the laws of attraction smoothly and without hitches.

Tips on How to Use the Law of Attraction to Become Successful

Here are a few tips to help you understand how you can get on the road to a better life:

- **Understand that your thoughts determine your vibration:**

A discussion about the Law of Attraction is difficult without talking about vibration. Thoughts cause a certain vibration. For example, if you consistently talk about how sick you feel, the Law of Attraction will sense sickness, and bring you more pain, more malaise and more symptoms.

On the other hand, if you talk about the well-being in your life, even if your current health is not that great, your vibration will begin to rise, causing the Law of Attraction to bring you circumstances and feelings that are closer to good health.

- **Using the Law of Attraction for gain, requires practice:**

It is very difficult to stop one way of thinking and then start another. The thought processes themselves do not change what the Law of Attraction brings to you. The Law of Attraction reads vibrations. Therefore, the vibrations must change.

The way to do this is gradually with practice, practice and more practice. Positive lasting changes come gradually, not overnight.

- **Long held beliefs change only with practice:**

Many people believe that whatever place they were born to, is where they have to stay. These beliefs come from intense conditioning throughout life. Very few of us understand the Law of Attraction, much less use it to our benefit. In not understanding this, we are subject to witnessing bad events and thus believing that things just happen to us at random.

This is the reason people tend to get stuck in certain places in their lives.

- **Associations need to change:**

As the Law of Attraction brings us according to our vibration, we find ourselves surrounded by people. These people often are similar in attitudes and beliefs. As you alter your thought processes to raise your vibration, you may find that your current relationships become uncomfortable. Friends may question, or even mock you about the changes you are making. Take heart.

As your vibration improves and better circumstances come into your life, friends will often be curious and want to join you in your journey. In addition, new people who match your new vibration appear.

- **You may need help:**

Changes in life, especially thought processes and beliefs, are challenging. In the beginning you feel vulnerable. You feel like you are in two worlds. Well-meaning friends and family may discourage you, causing you to give up.

The decision to engage a coach and join a community of likeminded individuals may mean the difference between building a wonderful life and staying in a place that is less than comfortable.

Conclusion

Basically, the law of attraction boils down to the concept and metaphysical belief that like attracts like. Man has always been searching for ways on how to manifest his dreams, wants and desires. The thing is that they do now know how to make it happen.

Before anything else, have you even wondered why this is called the law of attraction? Why is the word "law" used instead of "theory" if there is not enough scientific evidence to prove all its claims? Just like the law of gravity, the law of attraction applies to all. There are no selections and definitely, there are no selections.

Many are getting the misconceptions of the law of attraction. Many would say that they have always been positive, yet nothing has ever changed in their life. Many would say that they have always tried to think positively, yet the opposite tend to happen. The explanation to the law of attraction is plainly very simple. Allow me to cite a very common example.

If you think and say to yourself that "I need more money," you are stressing to yourself that you are "in need of more money." You are focusing on the problem and you are constantly repeating the "need" issue. Since the law of attraction only considers what is being emphasized, it will keep you in that state. Forever will you be stuck in that "need of more money" state if you are always focusing on the fact that you are in need of more money.

If the thinker changes his belief system the other way around to saying, "I am having more money," the thinker becomes what he thinks. Your system adapts the thought that you are having more money. With your focus and strong belief, you are releasing energy that will attract and manifest your thoughts. Remember that thoughts create emotions. Emotions will manifest actions. Actions will bring results.

Your dominant thoughts will find a way on how to manifest its entity. Your dominant thoughts will attract forces to make your belief happen. That's why, the mindset in the law of attraction is very important. Focusing and believing on what you want is critical. Being positive will give you positive results, likewise, being negative will bring you negative results.

Going back to the example mentioned above, because of the strong belief system that you have, you will deliberately find means and meet the best opportunity to make money. Suddenly, you will come to meet a good business opportunity, a high paying job, or with the best of luck, win a jackpot in the lottery or marry a billionaire. Of course, it is not just overnight. Sometimes, it might take a lengthy and painful process.

When you think you are giving up, remember what the law of attraction is all about. Always say to yourself that "I am attracting whatever I give my focus, attention and energy to, be it wanted or unwanted." So, do not spend your time contemplating about your problems, worries, concerns or how tired you have been.

Think that you can always do it because you are continuously moving anyway.

Here are 3 keys to give you a better understanding of the law of attraction:

- **Is a natural law:**

There are laws that govern the world we live in such as gravity, aerodynamics, and attraction. The law of attraction is a law that is in operation in your life whether you know it or not. It's just like gravity. You can pretend it doesn't exist but that doesn't change the fact that is does.

- **Like attracts like:**

Have you ever known someone that always seems to be successful? Some people may pass it off as just being lucky but that's not the case at all. Take a closer look at their life and you will see that they do the things necessary that attract success. The same goes for the person that seems like they are always failing. They are doing the things necessary to attract failure.

- **Change is the only answer:**

If you don't like what you are attracting in your life you are going to have to change. Take a look at your life and see what is holding you back from attracting what you want. You are going to have to be very honest with yourself. If you are and then make the necessary changes, you will see that you start to attract different things into your life.

Chapter Three

How A Scammer Always Ends Up With?

"Bread gained by deceit is sweet to a man, but afterward his mouth will be full of gravel." —Proverbs 20:17

How To Spot A Scam

This is a very brief description of a 419 scam and I will not even scratch the surface here. Several aspects of the 419 scam goes beyond the scope of this article and I plan to discuss them in future articles. The 419 scams (Four-One-Nine) got its name from the article of the Nigerian Criminal Code dealing with fraud.

Scammers often demand upfront payments for dubious reasons like processing fees, legal expenses or to bribe certain officials, therefore the scam also became known as Advance Fee Fraud. A 419 scam starts with an unsolicited e-mail from a scammer promising a huge sum of money, but the scammer will create the impression that you need to make a couple of upfront payments before you can lay your hands on this non-existent fund.

These upfront payments are normally a drop in the bucket, compared to the huge sum of money you will receive in the end. This makes the scam very attractive to unwary and uninformed people, who are desperate for some extra cash.

According to a report from the Federal Trade Commission (FTC), millennials are particularly more vulnerable to online scams than seniors, as shocking as it may seem. The research finds that "40 percent of adults age 20-29 who have reported fraud ended up losing money in a fraud case".

The Importance Of Spotting A 419 Scam

Prevention is the most important reason behind the successful identification of 419 scams, but this is not the only reason. Registrars, hosting companies, Internet Service Providers and Law Enforcement also need to familiarise themselves with the common characteristics of 419 scams, because their support and cooperation play a huge part in the battle against 419 fraud.

Unfortunately, many registrars and hosting companies fail to take a stand against the fraudulent activities of 419 swindlers. Registrars refuse to suspend the domains of known scammers and hosting companies fail to enforce their Acceptable Use Policies (AUP). There is a reason why registrars and hosting companies are hesitant to suspend the accounts of 419 scammers; Money!

These swindlers are their clients, so they are happy to host their fraudulent websites and support their spamming services. With some registrars unfortunately, you will never win, not even if you are Sherlock Holmes. They are simply ignorant to the 419 scam problem and do not care about the lives being destroyed by these scams.

To all the unethical registrars and hosting companies out there, don't tell me you have a hard time identifying Advance Fee Fraud websites, if you own a groceries store, will you knowingly sell Marijuana to your customers? Perhaps that was a stupid question. If you don't mind hosting a fraudulent website, you will probably have no problem selling Marijuana to your customers.

But what is the big difference here? If the cops catch you selling illegal drugs to the public, you can kiss your store goodbye, but it is a common misconception that the cops won't do a thing against a registrar who refuses to suspend the domain of a fraudulent website. The actual reason why registrars get away with murder is because complainants do not want to go through all the hassles of filing a complaint with the police and the cops sometimes do not have a clue how to approach a case like this, even if there are laws you can use to your advantage.

Yes, I am aware that your local police department won't have any jurisdiction over a webmaster in a foreign country, but even if they did, you are unlikely to get anywhere with a case like this, if you don't have deep pockets and the registrars know that.

I understand that registrars cannot go suspending domains left and right on a mere request or tip from the public, they have to conduct a thorough investigation before they can take any action. Abuse departments are swamped with fraud reports each day and on top of that I believe they get their fair share of false reports as well.

Members of the public need to get their facts straight before reporting a fraudulent website to a registrar, this improves the turnaround time of abuse complaints and makes the work of the abuse departments that much easier. I'm not saying you must conduct a full-scale investigation (unless you feel the need to do so), simply take the time to gather all the evidence and present the information to the abuse department in a logical and organised manner.

So many people resort to a quick e-mail like "Hey, check out this site, I think it is fraudulent." or "Hey, this guy sent me a fraudulent e-mail, and this is his e-mail address, please take him out". Good, you raised awareness about possible fraud, but tell the abuse department why you think the website is fraudulent.

Don't just send them an e-mail address of the suspect, send them a copy of the e-mail that was sent to you and don't just forward the damn thing inline, forward it as an attachment or include the full header of the e-mail along with the body. The abuse department will eventually find the e-mail address of the suspect in the copy that you sent to them.

Proper identification of 419 scams by members of the public will make these scams less effective and will eventually lead to a decrease in 419 activities. So let's take a closer look at the characteristics of a 419 scam.

What To Look For In A 419 Scam

- **The subject of the e-mail, as well as the name and e-mail address of the sender:**

By analysing the name and e-mail address of the sender in conjunction with the subject line of the scam e-mail, you can easily identify a 419 scam before opening it. Spotting a 419 scam at first glance minimises the risk of falling for the scam and saves you time (you don't have to read through all the mumbo jumbo of the scammer).

This also simplifies the task of reporting 419 scams to cyber security authorities.

Typical characteristics of subject lines, names and e-mail addresses used in 419 scams:

- Scammers love to disguise their true identity with the names of high profile figures like State Presidents, Ministers, Ambassadors, Directors, etc.
- Subject lines are often typed in uppercase letters only.
- They use free e-mail services like Yahoo, GMail, Hotmail/Live, or a free ISP e-mail account. These free e-

mail accounts are used in cases where one would expect an e-mail from an official e-mail address and surprisingly enough, there are still people who fall for this lame trick
- There is often an overdriven use of formal and professional titles like Mr, Mrs, Dr, Barr, Sgt., Lt, etc.
- Subject lines often have a false sense of urgency.
- The name of the sender is repeated in the subject line.
- Many scammers mistake the Subject for the From field and vice versa.
- Generic greetings like, "My Dear", "Dear Beloved", "Greetings to you", "Dearest Brother" or "Dear Sir/Madam" are sometimes used as a subject line.
- Many scammers are hypocrites who pretend to be devoted Christians and will use subject lines like: "Greeting In The Name Of Our Lord Jesus Christ", "My Dear Beloved In The Lord", "Goodness Of God Will Be Upon You", Or "You Are The Lord Chosen One".
- Subject lines contain notices about "Payments", "Lotteries", "Bank Drafts", "Compensation", "Funds" and other financial related terms.
- The subject line often contains an instruction to contact a specific individual, department or organisation. For example "Contact my secretary", "Contact the fiduciary agent", "Contact the bank official", "Contact the ATM Department of;" or "Contact FedEx".
- Scammers always come up with the strangest and most outrageous e-mail addresses, especially in scenarios where it is quite obvious that the e-mail account is fake. For example, a scammer pretending to be an official from the FBI will use a silly e-mail address like fbiofficial015@example.com. The FBI have their own domain and e-mail servers, so there is no valid reason for

- using an e-mail account from another domain, or a free e-mail service like Yahoo! or GMail.
- It is common practice among 419 scammers to use an e-mail address that consists of a formal title, a name and surname. For example, Mr. John Doe will use an e-mail address like mrjohndoe@example.com.
- It is very popular among 419 scammers to start their subject lines with the words: "From the Desk Of".
- Lottery scams often have a reference number for the subject line. For example "Award Notice (Ref: LSUK/2031/8161/05)"

This is not an exhaustive list of characteristics but is certainly a collection of the most common characteristics found in the subject lines, e-mail addresses and names of 419 scammers.

- **Questions you need to ask yourself before analysing a 419 scam any further:**

In order to answer these questions you need to open the e-mail and read its contents. At this point, you don't need to pay attention to specific details in the e-mail, you only need to determine what the e-mail is all about:

- Is the e-mail an unsolicited and unexpected job, loan or business offer from an unknown individual?
- Is it about a lottery or competition you never entered? (Remember: Having your e-mail address randomly drawn from a list does not count as a valid entry for a competition).
- Have you received a huge donation from a non-profit organisation?
- Are you appointed as the next of kin of a total stranger?

- Do need to help a foreigner to clear a consignment box, containing millions of dollars, declared as something else to a diplomatic courier service?
- Is the e-mail supposedly from an American Soldier, doing service in Iraq, who discovered millions of dollars and needs to get the money out of the country?
- Is the e-mail an unsolicited request to take care of orphans, send Bibles to a church or offer financial assistance to sick and hungry people in Africa?
- Are you appointed, as the beneficiary of a fund, where the owner of the fund is currently dying of cancer?
- Is the e-mail about the recovery of money or assets that were never stolen from you in the first place?
- Have you been awarded an unsolicited bank draft for your philanthropic efforts? Is the e-mail about an outstanding/delayed payment for a contract with some government, but you never entered into such an agreement or you never even conducted business with them at all?

If you answered YES to ANY of these questions, you are most definitely dealing with a scam.

Now ask yourself the following questions:

- Did you expect the e-mail?
- Do you know the sender in person?
- Did the sender mention your name in his/her initial e-mail?
- Does the sender have any other personal information about you (besides your name)? If so, did the sender supply a valid, trustworthy source of where he/she obtained the information?

If you answered NO to at least 50% of these questions, you are most likely dealing with a 419 scam.

Always remember the golden rule, if it sounds to good to be true, it probably is!

- **Analysing the contents of the e-mail:**

If the name and e-mail address of the sender, the subject line of the e-mail or the story of the sender leaves you clueless about the legitimacy of the e-mail, you will have to analyse the contents of the e-mail in greater detail.

The following characteristics are tell-tale signs of a 419 scam e-mail:

The Reply-To e-mail address is different from the originating e-mail address. Scammers do this to ensure they receive your reply, in case their service provider shuts down their e-mail account. Some scammers will spoof the "From" e-mail address with an official e-mail address.

If the sender does not provide a Reply-To e-mail address, he/she will specify an alternative e-mail address, in the body of the e-mail.

Sometimes the sender does not only provide a different Reply-To address, but also a completely different alias. The scammer wants to create the impression that you are sending your replies to a completely different person, but it is actually the same scammer operating both e-mail accounts, each one under a different alias.

The whole e-mail, or large portions of it, is typed in capital letters.

The e-mail starts with a generic greeting(as already discussed). Most scammers simply shoot in the dark when they distribute their scam e-mails, so they don't know your name and will therefore not mention it in the e-mail. (Never assume an e-mail is legitimate just because the sender knew your name. I have seen several 419 scam e-mails where the scammer already knew the name, last name and even the physical address of the recipient).

The sender pretend to care about the well-being of your family with greetings like: "Good Day, How are you today? I presume all is well with you and your family." Believe me, 419 scammers don't give a damn about your family, they are only trying to earn your trust by pretending to care. Other 419 scammers have an apologetic attitude right from the start, for example: "Dear, Please accept my sincere apologizes if my email does not meet your business or personal ethics".

The recipient of the e-mail needs to reply with personal details like his/her full name, telephone and fax number(s), residential address, birth date, gender, name and address of Next of Kin, banking details, occupation, marital status and nationality. Some scammers request a scanned copy of your photo ID, international passport or your driver's licence, so they are not only after a photo of yourself, they also want your identity number or social security number.

Scammers often request some ridiculous information from their victims. For example your e-mail address (they already made contact with you, why would they need your e-mail address again?), the country that you live in (even if they already asked for your residential address and/or nationality) or the amount of money that you won (in the case of a lottery scam).

The most common telephone numbers provided by 419 scammers are from South Africa (country code +27), Republic of Benin (country code +229), Nigeria (country code +234) and Netherlands (country code +31), but I've also seen telephone numbers from Sweden (country code +46), China (country code +86), Turkey (country code +90) and Malaysia (country code +60).

Scammers always put a lot of emphasis on keeping the knowledge of the prize money or inheritance fund strictly confidential. There is a good reason for this, they don't want you to talk to other people about this because someone might realise that you are being conned and inform you that the e-mail is a scam.

Scam e-mails contain loads of spelling errors and horrible grammar. However this is not a rule of thumb. Many 419 scammers have upped the standards and compose highly professional e-mails these days.

419 scams involve huge sums of money, but the victim normally shares in only a small part of this fund. However, the alleged fund is so huge that even a small percentage of the fund can mean millions of dollars for the victim. This makes the scam very attractive to the victims, even if they only get a small cut out of the deal.

Many 419 scammers create the impression that they have been in contact with you in the past and that they failed to transfer some huge fund to you on a previous occasion. It is really hard to believe that people will fall for such a lame story, because if you can't recall doing business with these idiots, why would you reply in the first place. This only proves that 419 scammers are capitalising on the weakness of greedy people.

419 scammers can sometimes be quite philosophical, for example they will say something like this in the introductory line of their scam e-mail: "This letter must come to you as a surprise, but I believe it is only a day that people meet and become great friends and business partners."

Characteristics Of Specific Types Of 419 Scams

Lottery Scams nearly almost have a line that reads something like this: ";winners were selected through a special internet ballot system from 40,000 individuals and companies E-mail addresses." Some Lottery scammers put it like this: ";draws was carried out through random sampling in our computerized E-mail selection machine TOTAL from a database of over 1,000,000 Email addresses drawn from all the continents of the world, and the Globe divided into Zones."

Most Lottery Scams have a silly disclaimer like this: "NOTE: You are to keep all lottery information away from the general public especially your Winning numbers. This is important as a case of double claims will not be entertained and will amount to disqualification of your already won prize."

In many Next of Kin Scams you miraculously have the same last name as the deceased, however the scammer quite conveniently forgets to mention the last name of the deceased in the initial e-mail. The trick here is to get the victim to reply with his/her personal information and then use the last name of the victim on the forged death certificate and relevant documentation.

Although it is not a rule of thumb, most Company Representative scammers offer 10% of their "income" to their victims. For some reason they like to use 10%, but I have seen scams where they only offer 5% and other, "more generous" scammers who offer up to 30%.

An Inheritance Fund Scam normally involves a corrupt banking official who allegedly stumbled across an abandoned account of a deceased billionaire, or it is someone who can't access the inheritance of a family member due to various reasons. The scammer often needs your help to get the money out of his/her country.

Inheritance Fund Scammers often provide links to news articles to back their facts (or should I say lies). For instance a scammer will use a plane crash as a basis for his/her story and provide links on a news site like CNN.com.

In a Bank Draft Scam, the scammer refers to a previous deal that failed and now you have to contact his/her secretary because he/she left you a bank draft and hasn't been able to send it to you, because he/she is busy with other "investment" projects.

Some Inheritance Fund Scammers pretend to send you the money via a pre-paid Visa or Maestro ATM card.

The Job Offer Scam normally involves a job in a foreign country, so the victim has to apply for a visa. This is how the scammers make their money. Victims have to pay a small fee to a certain company who will arrange the visa for them. I refer to a small fee because the fee is normally a little dust particle compared to the remuneration being offered to the victim.

The Compensation Scam often involves scammers who pretend to work for the United Nations or the FBI. These scammers pretend to compensate victims of 419 scams.

ATM Card Scammers pretend to be very kind by paying certain processing fees and a drug law clearance fee on your behalf. The drug law clearance fee is to certify that the money issued on your name, do not stem from any money laundering activities. This is only for the bluff and the scammers only try to give their victims peace of mind. They can cook up any bloody certificate, you will still be an accomplice in money laundering if you assist them in moving funds through your bank account.

419 scammers, using the story of the soldier in Iraq, who discovered a huge sum of money, always have some obscure plan to get the money out of the country. The most common one is transport via a diplomatic courier who has diplomatic immunity.

Several 419 scams about some kind of pending payment will state something like this: "…we were notified that you have waited for so long to receive this payment without success, we also confirmed that you have met all statutory requirements in respect of your pending payment."

Diplomatic Immunity Payment scammers often use the lame excuse that electronic fund transfers have resulted in payments being made to incorrect bank accounts, so they are shipping you the money in cold hard cash. These scams often contain a notice like this: "Note: The money is coming on 2 security proof boxes. The boxes are sealed with synthetic nylon seal and padded with machine." The scammers often claim that they declared the contents of these boxes as "Sensitive Photographic Film Material".

Some Inheritance Fund scammers allocate the funds in the ratio of 60% for the scammer, 30% for the victim and 10% for processing fees.

This is by far not a comprehensive list of 419 characteristics. Most of the specific details in this article will become outdated as time goes by. Today, many 419 scammers claim in their initial e-mail that they have paid the upfront fee on behalf of the victim. Many victims will bail out when the scammer mentions an upfront payment, so the effectiveness of these scams declined over time and the scammers had to improvise. However these fools will mention some kind of payment at some stage in the scam and vigilant people will bail out once again.

419 scammers never conform to any kind of standard, so it is hard to lay down a rigid set of rules for identifying 419 scams. 419 scams are just like any other kind of spam, there are millions of spammers out there, but a lot of these spammers use the same templates and techniques. After a while the templates and techniques become common knowledge and the spammers need to find new and innovative ways of infiltrating our mailboxes and our minds.

One thing that will keep up with the evolution of 419 scams is common sense. No one will ever be able to teach you all the tricks in the book, because there will always be at least one trick you didn't think of.

Reading between the lines, being vigilant and applying a bit of scepticism towards e-mails from an unknown source, can be a very effective weapon against online fraud.

The Fraud of Ponzi Schemes

While the world today is full of good, it is also full of lies and deceit where financial sharks lay in ambush for people to hand over their money to them. By following the trail of scams and scandals, I have found many concepts today similar to a Ponzi scheme which cheats people every day without them knowing.

Bernie Madoff is an American businessman from New York City, born in April 1938, and the former chairman of NASAQ, who recently admitted to running a massive investor fraud, also known as a "ponzi scheme". He founded the Wall Street investment firm, Bernard L. Madoff Investment Securities LLC in 1960 which was one of the largest in all of Wall Street.

Madoff was arrested soon after he confessed to his sons that he had swindled investors through an enormous Ponzi scheme in which he allegedly stole roughly $50 billion dollars of his investors' money. Prosecutors estimated losses of up to $65 billion. Madoff is currently looking at spending the rest of his life in prison and may be forced to pay a restitution of $170 billion.

What is a Ponzi Scheme?

Apparently, Bernie Madoff referred to his investment firm as a giant Ponzi Scheme, but what exactly does that mean? Well, according to the US Securities and Exchange Commission, the Ponzi Scheme Definition is a fraudulent investment operation that pays returns to investors using their own money or money coming in from future investors rather than from any legitimately earned money.

The Ponzi scheme is named after Charles Ponzi, who used this technique in the 1920s by paying investors a 50% return on short-term investments with money from later investors. Contrary to popular belief, Charles Ponzi was not the inventor of this type of scheme, but his operation became so infamous because of the amount of money involved that it became the first to be referred to as a "Ponzi Scheme" throughout the US.

While Ponzi Schemes are in fact illegal they continue to be discovered around the world, running on the "rob-Peter-to-pay-Paul" idea, as money from new investors is used to pay off previous investors in a continuous and destructive cycle until the entire fraud eventually collapses.

What to look for and How to Avoid a Ponzi Scheme Investment Fraud:

When looking to invest or start a new business, always be on the lookout for anything misleading. Do as much research as you can before getting involved and weigh out both the risks and the rewards. The potential business and/or investment should provide you with all pertinent information; if they are legitimate, they will have absolutely nothing to hide!

Seek out an honest and reputable company that will empower you with all the necessary information, mentoring and tools for both peace of mind and financial success!

How these scammers and fraudsters always end up

Karma has over time been said to mean action, work or deed; it also refers to the spiritual principle of cause and effect where intent and actions of an individual (cause) influence the future of that individual (effect). Good intent and good deeds contribute to good karma and happier rebirths, while bad intent and bad deeds contribute to bad karma and bad rebirths.

Given the natural cause and effect of Karma, we've witnessed for a while how scammers and fraudsters usually end up getting scammed, getting jailed or and up doing community service whilst paying back all the ill-gotten wealth they have accumulated back to their scam victims. Major examples that have bean headlined by various dailies are highlighted below:

1. On February 12, 2019, a gang of fraudsters based in South London who used compromised card details and "money mule" accounts to commit almost £200,000 of fraud have been sentenced to over nine years in prison at Southwark Crown Court. A total of ten defendants were sentenced in the case, with six of them receiving prison sentences and four of them receiving community orders.

The organised criminal gang conspired with Jason Yeboah, 25, a former NatWest employee who abused his position at the bank's branch in Norbury to provide customer details that were used to commit fraudulent transactions. Some of the fraud was committed by ordering new debit cards for accounts and then using them to take out cash. Large transfers were also made to young people across the UK who had been recruited as "money mules", allowing their accounts to be used to receive fraudulent funds and then withdrawing the money on behalf of the gang.

The fraud was spotted by investigators at NatWest who referred the case to the DCPCU. All victims were refunded.

Yeboah pleaded guilty to fraud by abuse of position and was sentenced to three and half year's imprisonment. Five members of the gang, all based in London (Simeon Adewale, Ougbenga Adubiyi, Temitayo Olaore, Jeff Adekoya and Alexander Ogun-Moweta) all received prison sentences of over nine months. One of these, Alexander Ogun-Moweta, 37, pleaded guilty to seven additional counts of fraud including conspiracy to buy a £65,000 Mercedes, and was sentenced to a total of 30 months in prison.

Four other defendants, who acted as "money mules" for the fraudsters and were based in locations across the UK including Bristol and Essex, pleaded guilty to possession of criminal property and received community orders including a total of 540 hours of unpaid work. "Money mules" are approached by fraudsters and asked to receive and send money through their own bank accounts, sometimes keeping some of the cash for themselves. Being a money mule is illegal, and when someone is caught their bank account will be closed, they will have problems getting student loans, mobile phone contracts and credit in the future, and they could get a criminal record.

2. A jailed fraudster has been ordered to pay back more than £570,000, or face a further term of imprisonment: 26 year-old Amuda Sheidu, who lived the high life on other people's money, is currently serving a 27-month jail term after admitting laundering £170,000 for an international crime gang. He was found by financial investigators to have reaped £578,632 from his criminal activity.

3. Two criminals from London who committed almost half a million pounds of fraud have received combined prison sentences of over 14 years following a successful investigation by the Dedicated Card and Payment Crime Unit (DCPCU), a specialist police unit funded by the banking and cards industry.

Desmond Amoako, 30, of Lakeside Drive, Brent, received a four-year prison sentence for conspiracy to defraud, a four-year prison sentence for money laundering and an eighteen-month prison sentence for possession of articles for use in fraud. All three prison sentences are to run concurrently.

Sami Ebraheem, 29, from Shoot Up Hill, Kilburn, was sentenced to two years and four months for conspiracy to defraud and another two years and four months for money laundering, also to run concurrently. A third defendant who helped facilitate the fraud, Ponle Odusina, of Mill Hill, London, received a suspended prison sentence of 12 weeks and 80 hours of unpaid work, after being found guilty of fraud by abuse of position. The three criminals were all sentenced on Friday 31 August at Blackfriars Crown Court.

Ebraheem and Amoako made hundreds of fraudulent transactions between 20 October 2017 and 25 October 2018, stealing a total of £457,000 from bank customers. The fraudsters first harvested bank details from customers using 'phishing' emails or 'smishing' text messages, before using 'sim swaps' to complete bank transfers and purchases on their accounts.

4. Tom Katona fell for the Nigerian bank fraud where he responded to the email of the "princess" "son" or "daughter" of the Nigerian government who would pay out twice the amount of money you pay in because they do not have access to American banks.

Mr. Katona decided not only to send in his life savings for the quick return, but he also sent in over a million dollars in county funds which he embezzled hoping to replace it all quickly when he cashed his Nigerian Cashiers Check, which of course, turned out to be fake.

'Woe to those who devise wickedness and work evil on their beds! When the morning dawns, they perform it, because it is in the power of their hand. They covet fields and seize them, and houses, and take them away; they oppress a man and his house, a man and his inheritance. Therefore thus says the Lord: behold, against this family I am devising disaster, from which you cannot remove your necks, and you shall not walk haughtily, for it will be a time of disaster. In that day they shall take up a taunt song against you and moan bitterly, and say, "We are utterly ruined; he changes the portion of my people; how he removes it from me! To an apostate he allots our fields." Therefore you will have none to cast the line by lot in the assembly of the Lord. ...'- Micah 2:1-3:12

Chapter Four

Successful People Often Have Great Ambitions And Dreams

Money. It's a word that can set even the most serious of people drooling. However much we have it, we crave for more. The presence is often equated to the assurance of happiness. We envy those who have it and wish we could be one of them. Who wouldn't love to be like a Carlos Slim or a Bill Gates, or at least own a part of their assets?

Yes, what wouldn't we do to be rich and affluent? But, it's not that easy to be rich. Or else there would be more of rich people in this world than the poor. After all, almost all our efforts and toils are aimed towards one aim and ambition - to earn money and become rich. So, if it's not easy, then how come there are rich people in this world? Where they all born rich? Definitely no. Then how did they become rich?

Well, let's check some of the mindsets and habits that can assure you financial affluence in life.

The Ability To Dream

Remember, first you have to visualize success before your actually attain it. Dream, and dream big. You may be a pauper of the worst sort. So what? After all, you don't have to pay any one for your dreams, right? Tell yourself that you are not going to stay in this rut forever. That, there will come a time when you would be out of it. Imagine what your life would be like when you become rich.

Naturally, when you tell your dreams to your friends there would be negative responses and efforts to dissuade you. So what? Everyone is entitled to their say. And you have the right to decide whether you should accept it or not. Remember, no one who has dreamt small has made it big. Even when circumstances don't work in your favour, don't give up on your dream.

Do you know that Thomas Alva Edison failed a whopping 10,000 times before he managed to make the electric bulb? Failures didn't dissuade him, nor did they destroy his dream. He hung on till success came his way. So dream, and never give up on your dreams till you have achieved them.

Failures, Don't Let Them Bog You Down

When J.K. Rowling wanted to sell her the first of her books in the Harry Potter series, 'The Sorcerer's Stone', no publisher in England was willing to put their money on it. They were positive that here was no market for books on magic. Rowling persisted, did not let the failures affect her, and stuck to her determination and the rest, as they say, is publishing history.

Now, just imagine if she had been bitterly disappointed by her lack of success, decided to give up and abandon her dreams? Well anyone who has read the Harry Potter series or watched the movie would admit that it would be equivalent to committing literary suicide and the world would have lost one of the most enduring and lovable fictional characters ever. The difference between the rich and the poor is basically, the difference in attitudes. No matter what happens, the rich - or those who are determined to succeed and attain financial affluence - do let failures affect them; since the rest of us are only too ready to give up at the mere shadow of failure.

Failures are just temporary setbacks. They are just hurdles that life throws our way to test our determination to succeed. When you learn to accept them in your stride, but do not let them deter you from your chosen path, success would naturally follow your efforts. Every time you fail, check your efforts to find out where you have gone wrong and why you have been rejected. Once you have analysed yourself, correct yourself before you move on to your desired goal.

Have Specific Goals And Pursue Them

Aimless journeys take you nowhere. They just take you back to where you had begun from. So, set goals for yourself. And remember, your goals should be attainable ones. For example, a 30 year old Indian national cannot aspire to become the President of America, right now, but someday in the future he will. Hence, make plans that are within your reach.

Think big but plan small. At least, in the beginning. Set short term goals for the initial stages. Of course, you should keep a bigger picture in mind of where you would reach in say 10 years of time. Once the goal is set, the next step involves setting the targets to attain that goal. How do you learn to ride a horse? First, you approach the horse and make sure that it has accepted you. Then you climb on it and learn to be comfortable in the saddle. Once that target has been achieved, you take a few steps to get the feel of the ride. Step by small step, you learn to be a rider.

Becoming rich is something similar to this. Your targets should be set for one step at a time. A cautious step is always better than a giant leap. Once you have become comfortable in your pursuit, step on the gas, and increase the speed. Pursue your goals with single-minded ambition. Here, we have a lot to learn from a child learning to walk. Cautious steps, followed by tentative effort and once the art has been mastered, there is no stopping them.

Choose Wisely

There are numerous ways out there to become rich. Different methods are suitable for different people. So, choose your path carefully. Identify your strengths and choose a profession where your skills can be used successfully. You know, John Keats' parents wanted him to be a surgeon. But Keats was sure that his talents lay in literary pursuits.

He abandoned his career in surgery halfway through and took to writing poetry. Of course, the way was strewn with boulders and storms; success was elusive; but he persisted and today is counted as one of the foremost Romantic poets of English language.

Grab your life by the scruff, be prepared for pitfalls and problems, have the courage to take risks and above all, dream big. And be happy in your richness.

Helping the vulnerable in the society

We all aspire to do good. It is the degree to which we want this that varies from individual to individual. To some, it comes naturally while others may need a little bit of encouragement to be more socially and environmentally responsible. Many corporate bodies engage in Corporate Social Responsibility (CSR) but we do not have to wait for the company to carry out a CSR for us to give back to our communities.

We can exercise social responsibility through efforts within our organizations or through acts of personal philanthropy or Individual Social Responsibility (ISR). ISR is where an individual becomes aware of how personal actions can affect others and the communities, we live in. Although it has been argued that ISR may sometimes be motivated by selfish reasons like social prestige or enhancement, it may also be done simply for the need to belong or for meaningful existence. I believe the benefits far out way the negatives in this case.

The giving may be quite lopsided towards a more visible initiative or target group, but it can be argued that the recipients will still be that much better off, and the benefits will have a trickledown effect.

Many times, people who have been on the receiving end of a CSR or ISR end up becoming motivated to do good as well. They tend to 'Pay it forward'. (This is described as the concept of asking that a good deed be repaid by having it done to others instead.)

The CEO of every business is a chief encouragement officer not a fierce disciplinarian. It is a known phenomenon that if you desire success in any spheres then it shall behove you to help others to succeed thus it shall follow that you shall succeed too. It may actually behove managers to train their own replacements as this has a certain form of loyalty not otherwise attained. After all everyone wants to advance and surely the manager wants to as well otherwise dormancy descends and jealousy.

'My sheep wander over the mountains and high hills; and when they are scattered throughout the land, no one bothers about them or looks for them.' - EZEKIEL 34:6

Being in a mastermind group opens up a different world of opportunity and as we desire to attract success then we need something that covers a broader gamut than any other and this theme generates a range of possibilities.

When Edison's factory burned down Ford arrived the next morning and gave him a check for $750,000 to rebuild and start all over again. This is what I mean by having the right team and with it success will be inevitable and marvellous. We have to think big as big as we possibly can for it is only by thinking big, we can accumulate the driving energy to surpass expectations.

Trust is the most important ingredient of the mastermind group and that everything discussed within the meetings remains within the meetings. There are no outside discussions about any subject. The success of every member depends on this vital element for creativity to flow and objectivity to remain.

The first mastermind group was Jesus and his apostles which was enlarged upon by Peter and Paul and their successors. Masterminds are ultimately about contributing to the success of others in the process of finding your own solutions, taking action and moving closer to your goals and dreams.

Masterminds are not the same as networking. As Napoleon Hill says: 'The coordination of knowledge and effort of two or more people who work towards a definite purpose in the spirit of harmony.' Napoleon was a current era founder of the Mastermind concept in his book Think and Grow Rich. One of the key elements of Hill's philosophy was to draw upon the spiritual forces within you.

'One outstanding element of the mastermind group brings focus on what I was saying earlier, and it is this. Something like a group intuition develops and it takes on a life of its own. Some describe it as an intelligence that is beyond themselves. It is an exponential intellect that can never be achieved by an individual separately.'
NH

There are no excuses for the failure of the mastermind's attendance record to be anything but regular if success is truly to be attained. When compiling the team this is an important element in choosing the members based on experience and intuition. Do not build your team with friends alone as that is a recipe for disaster and in fact unless any family member shows outstanding support for you in all creative ideas shut them from your minds. When considering who to include choose your purpose. Look for people who aspire to the same level of achievement; or higher. Assess if they are willing to explore new ways to conduct their lives and business.

Successful masterminds are built on trust, honesty, authenticity, vulnerability and the willingness to risk with each other. Even one member with questionable integrity will compromise the entire group, diminishing the shared trust and therefore the level of risk or vulnerability people are willing to explore with each other. We have seen this in many facets of society from business to committees to ministerial brethren.

> How committed are you to reach your objective and then based on your burning desire?

A True Story

When I was just out of school and in my early twenties, I met a multi-millionaire who ran a variety of successful businesses. I asked him if there was a secret to his success.

"Son," he said, "there are many secrets, but the biggest of them all -- it's bigger than the Empire State Building and the Sears Building in Chicago combined -- is more important than anything you can think of. It's the very bedrock of society. You've heard of the ladder of success, haven't you?"

"Yes, Sir," I said.

"Well, the ladder of success is made of relationships! And," he whispered, "Treat everyone you meet like a child . . . and you'll go places!'

"A child?"

"A child."

"Everyone?"

"No exceptions!"

At the time, I didn't see it, but over the years I have come to see the truth in what he was saying. After doing counselling, coaching and consulting, for nearly three decades, I can tell you how right he was!

- **What Was He Saying?**

All of us are really children in disguise. All ogres, big bad wolves, all crooks and vampires, all swindlers, saints and do-gooders, all statesmen, parents and teachers of any kind, all scientists, funeral directors and centenarians, all musicians, actors and wimps are children . . . everyone on earth is a child inside.

- **How Does It Help?**

It's simple and effective. The magic of creating and sustaining incredibly successful and enjoyable relationships begins with this knowledge. Just remembering it is the first step toward success; remembering that these children in your life want to be valued, adored and loved, and they crave respect, attention and acknowledgment.

As soon as you forget about them, they'll get ticked! So, all you have to do is supply the need. Give them what they want. When you do so, they will attach great affection and importance to you. You'll not only be well liked, but you'll enjoy their support when you need it.

Each of your relationships will prosper if you develop a consistent habit of giving the relationship what it needs to thrive, within reason, of course, treating each person in your life as though he is special.

Give everyone the understanding and patience you would give to a child. Treat every single person like you would a child who has the potential of growing up someday and doing great things in the world. Give your love, support and encouragement. Be patient and understanding. Never lose your temper with a child, never embarrass or mistreat a vulnerable child.

That's right . . . we're all vulnerable. Think about it, if a child is beautiful, what do you do? You say, "What a beautiful child, or what lovely eyes or hair you have!"

But with adults, we are often less open and expressive. I have learned to give compliments and kudos freely, even at the risk of being misunderstood. I love making people feel good. I love touching people's lives in caring ways. I have learned to go out of my way to give words of encouragement or congratulations. It feels so good!

People will brag on a child to his face, but seldom will they do the same for an adult. I have learned to see the beautiful child that resides in everyone, and by appealing to that child and respecting it, I am often able to forge partnerships and alliances which one might think impossible.

You can do the same. Put this idea to work for you by always finding the beautiful, lonely or talented child in everyone, and finding some way to recognize, inspire or celebrate the beauty therein.

Remember my formula for terrific relationships:

- Art (Creativity)
- Constant effort
- Knowledge and skill
- Treat everyone you meet like a child

All Children:

- Are easily hurt, and prone to bouts of moodiness, despair and ill-logic
- Sometimes think only with their hearts
- Behave like spoiled brats at least once in a while

Accept these realities, treat all people as children and give them the dignity and respect they deserve or need, and you will be famously effective with people of all kinds . . . and you will be a huge success!

How To Be A Leader Shaped Leader To Be A Highly Effective Leader For The Vulnerable Society

"Personal Proficiency + Professional Mastery = A Leader Shaped Leader"

How do ordinary people manifest humility to achieve significant Personal Proficiencies that deliver extraordinary results?

They remain on a continuum for learning to achieve greatness, become an agent of change through positive organizational behaviours and establish a leadership signature that links their leadership to their legacy.

Most importantly, when the unexpected happens and the results are less than expected, they carry the pains and burdens upon their shoulders without blame to others - relying on a Memorandum of Understanding - the collective behaviours and cultural influences from the trusted people, their teams, within their employ.

The Leader Shaped Leader

The Leader Shaped Leader sits atop a hierarchy of six significant leadership and organizational behavioural stages - and possesses the skills of all six. Individuals without these skills have gaps in their understanding of producing exceptional leadership for the 21st century and beyond.

Perhaps the most important component in the transition from ordinary to extraordinary is what our faculty calls, the "Process of Leader Shaping: the 'intellectual and emotional thought space' for value creation."

- **Stage One:**

Is the "Recruit, the good-to-great highly capable individual who makes productive contributions through talent, knowledge, skills and good work habits. This individual is the one person in the environment that understands 'people first, then the organization;' hence, the development and achievement of the desired effects within the expected Future Picture."

- **Stage Two:**

Is the Experienced Manager "who is working to establish his/her 'Leadership Signature' to integrate their newly found skills to the achievement of team and organizational objectives (mission) and work effectively with others in a team-led environment. The Experienced Manager begins his/her growth by learning the constructs in the Memorandum of Understanding to find a voice; then, influences others to find theirs."

- **Stage Three:**

Is the competent Fleet Leader who "understands the criticality of employing organizational behaviour across environments - organizes people and resources to develop an effective strategy forward using the critical Centres of Gravity to achieve the desired effects."

- **Stage Four:**

Is an effective Breakthrough Executor who "outlines the specific cognitive abilities that will be sought and cultivated by other leaders in the years ahead using the Five Minds for the Future: the disciplined mind, the synthesizing mind, the creating mind, the respectful mind, and the ethical mind; the leader who remains committed to a vigorous pursuit of a clear and compelling vision, stimulating higher performance standards using team manoeuvres."

- **Stage Five:**

Is the Team/Project Leader who "employs the highest standards of customer service by achieving the five disciplines of greatness - these are the leaders who understand manoeuvre warfare and the disciplines within a Five Paragraph Order: SMEAC. They know an extraordinary organization is one that is driven by extraordinary people who make a distinctive impact and deliver superior performance over a long period of time - as a team unit."

- **Stage Six:**

Is the Leader Shaped Leader "who employs organizational strategic execution tactics (The OrgSx Paradigm) to permeate enduring greatness through a paradoxical blend of personal humility and professional will. All successful organizations have a single component in common; they have a strategic-executor at the helm who knows the disciplines of 'strategic agility' and 'flawless execution.' These leaders are described as being tactical in their approach, ferocious and fearless, yet modest with an unwavering commitment to high standards." This is the leader who knows how to win!

A synonym for "Fearlessness," Leader Shaping provides the cultural influences and the collective behaviours used for facing the reality of your current situation, to recognize what you can actually achieve given the powerful organizational and relationship dynamics without thinking that you can actually achieve success through your own will, and become more powerful than you are.

And then, at the same time, while moving equal amounts of energy from the depths of your character, you decide who you want to be, so that you can stand firm on personal conviction and the practices of life that you believe most deeply in, so as to accept criticism and achieve greatness. This is the beginning stage within an expected healthy debate about the nature and effectiveness of employing transformational thinking and change across organizations that is seeking to achieve a well-planned Future Picture for generations to follow - greatness requires a Leader Shaped Leader for influencing the same from others and from within the growing organizations they are a part.

Making It Happen: Living The Work, Doing The Story For The Glory!

In this day and time, there are some people who are willing to have the glory before the story. Let me be the first to say that this is the wrong thinking that results terrible outcomes. Nothing in life, and certainly not in leadership, comes easy. Having the story before the glory prepares anyone for the tough road ahead and allows for the proper amount of "humility" along the way.

A question to ask yourself and those individuals who trust in your leadership is this: what do we do to prepare our people, our teams and our organizations for uncertainty - a plan for the future that exceeds everyone's expectations? The answer is a complex, yet simple one; keep pace with today's rapidly changing business environment by engaging and improving your emotional intelligence and organizational behaviour skills to recognize, adopt and adapt generational expertise, to include concepts of team-building practices and high-performance perception and values that result realistic winning solutions into the future.

Are you ready to challenge yourself to a higher purpose of leadership?

Taking on a leadership role in today's environment is like signing on for a constant race against change. You have to stay several steps ahead of the trends;strive to develop new strategies and keep ahead of the crowd. It's up to you to ensure that your department or team is on track for success. And now you can achieve your leadership goals!

Here is your opportunity to learn how to identify and manage the challenges you face with practical and proven-in-action techniques. The following information explains what it takes to become a "Leader Shaped Leader." In-class exercises, coupled with updates on current research and performance management assessments, allow you to practice new ideas, military stratagem, gaming/simulation and to try out shared insights. In this highly interactive executive education program, participants will have the opportunity to learn from their team associates and peers as they stretch their leadership driven minds and methods for learning to assert their role upon return to their workplace, organization and home life.

Leader Shaping as a Philosophy

In general, philosophy is the search for sense, meaning, cause and principle using logical thinking and rigorous thought. Philosophy unearths foundations and stresses being and mechanisms, discerning what things are and how they work. It is an attempt to perceive what things really are, not how they appear to be, and to discern how things really work, not how they appear to work. Philosophy seeks ultimate, irreducible truth.

Philosophy claims to be able to make sense out of any human awareness or endeavour, however massive or minuscule. Perhaps we will find interesting things about the nature of investing in humanity. But how? The answer lies within the Process of Leader Shaping's hierarchy of six significant leadership and organizational behaviour stages.

As you think about how individuals are by nature, you quickly realize how selfish people really are. They consider their own actions first: How will this affect me? At the same time, we try to disguise our selfishness with an authentic portrayal of interests that ultimately show its true face that leads to problems. This brings us to the alpha and omega on influence. It is important to acknowledge an individual's ability to get along well with others while achieving their cooperation and shared-vision for reaching mission objectives and assigned tasks.

By defining the differences between "leadership" and "management" (this is still, to some, confusing phenomena) as the prior and "Leader Shaping" as the ladder, we can identify noteworthy differences and commonalties, clarify what Leader Shaping includes that the other omits, and identify significantly fruitful ways that a marriage of the three can engender an interesting new concept or philosophy.

Leadership is frequently defined as the ability to exercise influence across a group or team of people with the expectations of meeting the mission objectives established for the future. The ability to exert such influence can derive formally from one's position, office, title, function, control of resources, control of rewards and punishments, or role; or informally from one's abilities, skills, experience, expertise, behaviour, style, charisma, or charm. A given leader may have at his/her disposal either or both formal and informal sources of influence, but it remains his/her potential to manage them to decide just how successful they are as a leader. Regardless of the level of influence, a social relationship exists.

There are two forms of social relationships to consider; one with people and the other with the environment. So far, we've spoken about the people aspect, but the relationship with the environment, also known as "Social Learning Theory: the reciprocal relationships between behaviours and environments," focuses in the area of "Organizational Behaviour: the study and application of knowledge about how people, individuals, groups and teams act in organizations, while being influenced by others." It does this by interpreting people/organizational relationships in terms of the whole person, whole group, whole team, whole organization, and whole social system. Its purpose is to build better relationships by achieving human objectives, organizational objectives, and social objectives. As you can see from the explanation above, the study of organization behaviour encompasses a wide range of topics, such as human behaviour, change, leadership and management, teams, execution and more.

It is important to be aware that leadership does not exist in a social vacuum, but rather is socially defined and determined in terms of one's influence on others. Leadership only exists if there is someone to be led who accepts the leader's influence in order to attain a goal, while management is all about managing process. Leadership, by its very nature, is an entity of influence through choice and changing environmental reality. As we think about popular culture and its belief for what leadership may be, the conclusion would bring most individuals to the conclusion (and not an assumption) that there is a greater state that achieves leadership itself. Leadership focuses on the long-term, but management places its focus on the short-term.

Leadership keeps its eye on the horizon, while management keeps its eye on the bottom-line. Leadership will tolerate failure or missteps as long as the direction provides instruction toward the goal for both the individual and the organization to learn from the failure or the lessons learned.

Failure, therefore, is viewed as a significant opportunity to learn - only when it is managed and turned into a precise process. It is therefore safe to say that when thinking about how individuals comprehend an ability to influence environments to become successful at meeting its objectives, it would be OK to acknowledge the current state of leadership does not fit into a single mould. There are six characteristics that provide a framework for people in leadership that helps them to achieve a state of understanding for its being. By gaining a thorough understanding for the framework's place, the six characteristics define the leader's intent and builds his/her level of trust with others - the framework is also the core discipline that increases credibility across the environments that leadership has a significant presence.

The six characteristics within the framework are known as the 6Cs: Consistency, Courage, Conviction, Commitment, Contrite, and Captivating.

- **Consistency:**

Leaders steadily act to influence greatness. They achieve all accomplishments through collaboration by fostering a warrior culture and the ultimate obligation of a winner rather than an uninspired drive that results significant under-achievement.

- **Courage (Challenge the Established Processes):**

Leaders must never run from doing what is right. They must be prepared to step out on faith, removing themselves outside of popular culture, while searching for the courage and understanding to win over failure. This characteristic is where the rainmakers reside.

- **Conviction:**

Leaders communicate their convictions boldly.

- **Commitment (Model the Way):**

Leaders understand that the only thing necessary for the triumph of greatness is for the chosen to fail at not trying! Allowing your walk to mirror your talk demonstrates by example "what" should be done and "how" it must be done to execute task and responsibilities strategically and flawlessly.

- **Contrite (Encourage and Inspire the Heart of a Winner):**

Leaders know when to be humble and willingly demonstrate ability for being flexible in their way of thinking, hence transformational thought. Be prepared to recognize, appreciate, and celebrate the contributions from all persons involved in the winning process.

- **Captivating (Inspire a Shared-Vision):**

Leaders are tactical in their ability to positively influence a journey within the community that helps the stakeholders to find their voices. Individuals must envision the future picture that includes a sense of vitality and creativity that appeal to the desires of all stakeholders who act and contribute to the realization of an established vision.

The characteristics that make-up this framework for leadership helps individuals to become the maverick conformists that stimulate a community's ability to change its perspective to current reality, using best practices, when needed. As time matriculates as a changing paradigm, so does a vision and the expected outcomes within an environment of trust. And, as this happens, an individual in a position of leadership will assert or affirm positive influence that transfers an attitudinal approach for achieving excellence to others within their community. In doing so, recognition is achieved at all levels and places individuals on a continuum for future examination of proactive change.

Here are some other things about leadership for consideration. Leadership must reinforce the values of the mission outlined by positive organizational behaviour. Because all actions are based on internal and often unexpressed motivation and behaviour, leaders recognize that achieving buy-in from their associates is the way to success.

In contrast, management focuses exclusively on the actions and behaviours of their associates with little or no interest in the reasons behind those actions. One of the greatest attributes for effective leaders is that they are unafraid of looking vulnerable to their peers when they don't have the answers that others are seeking. In the same light, some managers when they don't have the answers to the information tend to place emotional distance between themselves and those seeking the information. Leaders will listen to the people around them, knowing that they may glean lessons from their peers.

Old school managers were known to talk at the people, thinking that they cannot learn from people who may not be on their level. Leaders quickly and effectively learn to openly embrace diversity and multiculturalism, while managers might try to encourage traditionalism. Effective leaders inspire the heart of a winner, while a manager may focus exclusively on the mind of a player. Leaders will courageously embrace change if they feel that change is eminent for the system to experience growth.

Managers will have a difficult time overcoming resistance to change and might hold the reins tightly to preserve the status quo. Leaders inspire and develop emotional bonds to the mission at hand, but managers will tend to create compliance issues and stick closely to the status quo that might lead to a commanding perspective. Leaders create, inspire, and support idealization within their peer groups, while managers dictate based on the inflexible approach to leading.

Leadership, therefore, is crucial in creating exceptional performance. Leadership and management skills are complementary. Leadership combined with management creates synergistic opportunities and engage the mind, body, heart, and soul of the associates influenced by the actions of a winning team of great leadership qualities and positive influence. Leadership is the successful influence of management in human behaviour in and away from the environment. Those chosen to lead lay foundational structure for the leaders they develop and influence to no longer just give words to lofty, ethical values; now they are required to walk the talk and deliver at high performance levels with significant implications for effective results.

Success into the future requires not only leaders who can manage, but managers who can lead systems, people, and environments into greatness, only now, at a much higher level. The people who are able to accept "command" as the exercise of authority and "control" as feedback about the effects of the action taken. This is the outcome and most significant difference from those who are Leader Shaped and the people who are not.

A discipline of leadership that works to develop an intense, custom learning experience used to understand leadership and management to increase the leadership ability - personally and professionally - in people seeking a better tomorrow means that a process must be endured. This is a process that helps individuals to drive fundamental change and to achieve communal commitment by applying a unified framework of understanding a significant body of knowledge - the body of knowledge that encapsulates leadership, management, organizational behaviour, team building and strategic execution - hence, the essential and key disciplines in Leader Shaping!

In addition to what has been explained thus far, Leader Shaping too, inspires and encourages a shared-vision of making "deposits" and "withdrawals" that both profit individuals and organizations and creates winning attitudes within the race of change. There are several questions to consider here: how would one go about creating new paradigms to current reality and norms? How do you overcome resistance to change? A third issue to examine is the outcome of the Future Picture (a state that you intend to make happen as a successful platform for forward motion or an end-state). How do you stimulate change and own it as a requirement for transitioning your life, relationships, teams, or organizational development? The answer to these questions lie in your ability to comprehend the profound implications of both the social aspects in leadership and the centurion principles that each Leader Shaped Leader possesses: a rise throughout the ranks of leadership while demonstrating exceptional mental sharpness and discipline, and physical endurance to understand and deal with the strategic and tactical thought ;and it all comes at a cost; "emotional restraint, sweat and sacrifice."

An interesting state of affairs exists between leadership, management and Leader Shaping - people, both as followers and leaders themselves, and the complex dance along the way. To be an effective leader, an individual must possess certain qualities or certain sources of influence that other people do not possess. They seek to readily employ these qualities as credible resources to address various burning platforms before they flare up when required or needed.

In a sense then, a leader is someone who differs from all others. If leadership was easy, more people would be doing it and recruited for it. However, when you add the additional ingredients that are needed for the 21st century and beyond, Leader Shaping, the leader must perform a very difficult balancing act, to be like their followers, but also to behave differently than their followers. Expressing this balancing act in a somewhat different manner, a leader must be in front of followers, (no longer leading from the flanks, rear or middle) taking people from an ordinary group to an extraordinary team, where they must want to journey or be influenced to go.

Leader Shaped Leaders must be able to do the following, much different from leaders:

- Transform their way of thinking from simply thinking outside of the box; they must have the know-how to bury the box and be damn certain that the enemy cannot find the box and dig it up.
- Understand that failure is the greatest teacher; "victory" instructs the simple, "failure" the wise; success teaches few lessons, but failure teaches many. Debrief for lessons learned and learn from them - the failures that is!
- Know "how-to" use fresh ideas, hone them for efficient and effective integration, and model for reproduction using the ideas as the basis for modelling to learn, teach, and lead into the future: Instruct a shared-vision by influencing trust through balance; Demonstrate by example the benefits and features found in success; Experience the glory after executing process and procedure flawlessly; and Assess all areas of the environment to reshape and reconfigure process to ensure enduring success.

- Understand the know-how for using the Seven "D's" of Courage: (1) Desire: Become a champion of change; a major part of a solution; (2) Dream: Achieve a preferred future picture with just leaders; (3) Decisiveness: Recognize the process of trust, competence, and influence to encourage and inspire a journey to find your voice; (4) Dare: The courage to act outweighs the fear to not! (5) Dedication: Remain committed to fulfil the responsibility within a call; (6) Direction: Achieve a clear plan of influenced and proactive change; and (7) Dependence: Rely on achieving greatness - not effectiveness.

- Transfer the knowledge and use of the "The Morale Constructs Strategy." The secret to building a shared-vision across an organization is to get the associates to think less of their motives and more of the mission at hand. Achieving this measure requires trust, credibility, character, and an understanding of your situational awareness at all times. Ensure the members of the community each understands the competitive forces against the system and the potential outcome should the forces breach the talent fields of the organization. Turn the mission into a crusade that everyone is a major influence to narrow the competitions base of support and room for tactical manoeuvring. Always lean on "right," as the good guy's white hat never hits the ground due to his convictions and disposition for righteousness.

You now have before you the opportunity to take the steps that achieve a high level of personal mastery for your life. It requires the adoption of a "code" as a living organism into your life. How can you build awareness, use your experiences in implementing a new approach to deportment, and develop a strategy, which includes resolve and ethical conduct? This is the task before you.

It sounds like the normal work that we all know and do so well. But be cautioned, it is not! When we bind the code with rules and regulations, reporting and accountability to force conformity to standards, we will fail - to oppose change by way of fear is not what we want. Rather, achieving personal mastery is a continuous, yet discontinuous pursuit of ethical behaviour that ultimately manifests into a quest of improving the human spirit; to pursue good, to do the right thing in our lives, work and in the workplace. The code says that whoever should adopt it into his/her life, will possess a level of courage - both physically and emotionally - to execute the necessary task that drives performance that exemplify the highest level of personal conviction.

Chapter Five

Why Do You Really Need Leadership Skills To Effect Changes?

It is a well-known fact that most people believe that leaders are born, not made. It is also an unfortunate belief that those who have leadership potential also believe this as truth.

However, the others believe that leaders can be made. There are those with charisma and the needed confidence to be leaders to the point they stand out as role models in many facets of society. Depending on work positions and a number of other factors these individuals are missing out on a grand slice of life and with just a bit of leadership training they might easily fulfil their role as society leaders.

Why is leadership so important today?

Mother Teresa once said 'We can do no great things, only small things with great love'.

If we are to create positive change and make a difference in our world, we must begin with ourselves. There are two keys that are crucial to celebrating difference in yourself and others:

- Your willingness to change and
- Willingness to face your fears of difference

The first key is a willingness to change. Being different involves change. Change is always desired intellectually. However, the emotional experience of change requires that we feel chaos and uncertainty. Most people are afraid of chaos and recoil from it, thus resisting real change. All genuine change produces chaos; the bigger the change the greater the chaos. Remember that once the changes are made the chaos will subside and empowerment will prevail.

Commitment is a condition where you not only take responsibility for your actions but also assume the care and conditioning, failures and success of others. But it does require some action which has to be driven by an internal motivation. Once the decision is made to become a leader, the training will reinforce that decision towards reaching its fullest potential.

As humans, we ensure as much as possible to seek happiness in everything we do. Leadership skills allows you to act out your compassion and kindness. Compassion and kindness bring out happiness.

Leadership is not only demonstrated by mobilizing the masses and impacting nations. It is demonstrated by a change of heart, to cultivate a willingness to address injustices. The changing of heart to be sensitive for opportunities to make a difference makes leadership something very personal. If the change does not start with the individual, if you cannot lead yourself to do the right thing, you can lead no one else!

Having leadership skills is important in making an impact in this world and also in order to be successful and have a big impact or to change system that you have pain with, we all need help from other human beings. We are socializing animals. All successful people need to help from other people.

It is becoming a fact that leaders consistently do things that others don't — they lead by example. Their ability to bring out the best in people around them can seem effortless. Leaders are knowledgeable, curious and empathetic, but also serious and committed to what they believe in, and that includes the people they work with.

The great thing about leaders is that their ability to inspire others to do their best increases engagement. When working with leaders, people often don't know that they're giving more than their usual until they find themselves doing things to better their own game.

To handle daily life challenges, we need leadership skills to find opportunities in a difficult situation. Leadership provides new opportunities to others such as jobs and income opportunities. Leadership is about leading by example. To achieve daily life goals even to do list, we all have to depend on our leadership skills. Leaders have their own logic; they do not follow the crowd.

And the sense of responsibility in works and ethics make us more successful and inspire others to follow.

Example of leadership in everyday life:

- When you complete your to-do list each day, it is an example of leadership
- When housewives or parents or I or you take responsibility to prepare food for kids; that is leadership
- When you think about pollution in the environment and think to reduce or clean pollution from your area, and you take action towards it is leadership
- When you guide, command, inspire others to follow the right path to become successful in career and business, it is leadership
- When everyone is saying, that this is not possible, we can't do that, there are so many problems, then one individual or team come up with an idea, come with a solution; that is leadership. He/she show the path or

- ways to grab this opportunity, they plan and then they create executable plans and process
- Leadership is like providing your seat to elders or female's passengers in the bus
- Leadership is when you take charge of your success and failure and in life

The happier you are, the more likely you are to experience success as a leader. Happiness has a compounding effect because happiness – which has its origins in personality and past successes – leads to behaviours that in turn lead to future success.

When you are with people who are happy, they build you up, not drag you down. Their happiness is usually infectious. You can choose to put in place practices to make yourself happier. It's like a plant. For it to thrive it needs to be nourished, watered and cared for. So too for your happiness quotient.

Some gems because of their sheer presence and charisma and whether or not these people use their talent for good things has always been a nature vs nurture debate. But the world has seen many great leaders in all the parts of the world but some of the leaders have had not only an influence on their own countries but on the world.

Here are a few of the world's greatest leaders:

❖ **Mahatma Gandhi**

Born an ordinary boy Mohandas Karamchand Gandhi, he later became known as the Father of the Nation or 'bapu'. Mahatma Gandhi led India against the tyrannical rule of the Britishers. He fought silently and practiced ahinsa or non-violence. He believed that truth and only truth shall prevail and without harming a single soul, he got freedom to India. Civil disobedience movements, boycotts of foreign goods etc is how he showed his resistance towards the British. Eventually, The British left India and Gandhi became the face of the nation. He is, without doubt, one of the greatest leaders to have ever walked the earth.

- **Nelson Mandela**

No one needs an introduction for this great man. Nelson Mandela was the first democratically elected President of South Africa. He was the leader and the face of the Anti- Apartheid movement and all through his life, he relentlessly fought against racial discrimination. For his actions, he served a long prison sentence but even that did not deter him. He came out as a hero and led the country into a free, equal future. His determination, focus and will-power were tremendous that even after serving almost 30 years in jail, he got out and worked again for what was right.

- **Martin Luther King Jr.**

It all started with a dream, like it always does. A dream for change and a dream for better tomorrow. Martin Luther King Jr. was an activist and a leader in the civil rights movement of USA. He was also a member of the clergy. He is known for the non-violent ways in which he advanced and led the civil rights movement. He fought for racial equality and showed the people a picture of a better future where all men are equal. Courage, perseverance and the will to fight for what's right till the very end made him a great leader. He won The Nobel Peace Prize in 1964.

How To Be More Compassionate As A Leader

Passion: a strong and barely controllable emotion is a feeling of intense enthusiasm towards or compelling desire for someone or something. Passion can range from eager interest in or admiration for an idea, proposal, or cause; to enthusiastic enjoyment of an interest or activity; to strong attraction, excitement, or emotion towards a person.

Passion is your fuel. It motivates you to press on. It propels you up the mountain of your dreams and goals. Someone who is passionate is intriguing to watch and to listen to. They are usually energizing to be around.

Passion draws people in, and to you. They want to be part of that passion. They want to be motivated as you are. They want to touch that passion and embrace it. Passion lifts people up to a

new level, which they can feel for themselves and from you. Passion encourages and whips new energy into people and projects. Everyone wants to feel passion for something.

When you come to roadblocks in life, your passion is what brings you beyond each and every halt.

Remember, small things can become big dreams if you are passionate about them. Take care of the small details with the same care and regard as if it were a great big event and you will move up the mountain with a steady sure foot.

Passionate leaders recognize passionate people, and the details of passion, and they hire and promote passionate workers, and create openings for those people.

As a leader, many times you cannot do things on your own, and that is when your passion will lead you to a partner or a team with your same passion that can help you. Now you can do it together as a team that is as passionate for your goals as you are. You and them become stronger as you work together.

Now the team has developed a reputation of excellence and passion. You will see that more creative and energetic people are drawn to the team because they like what they are seeing. Because of that, your team will be able to do more than they could before, and do more awesome projects. Your team will be able to scale impossible heights in a very short period of time, and perhaps you will reach the greatest pinnacles of success that you have ever dreamed about.

How to find your passion

1. Write a list of what excites you:

This includes things you've done, experiences, desire or maybe simply think you want to experience. (Remember, you don't know what you don't know. This means there are likely a lot of things you don't know about at this point that could excite you tremendously).

2. What, or maybe who, fills you with passion?

What inspires you, drives you to take action. This could be a cause, an example someone has set, a dream;

3. Write down an inexhaustive list of the things you do NOT want in your life:

This includes the type of person you do NOT want to be.

4. On a new sheet of paper, for each item in #3, write down the opposite, exactly what it is you DO want.
5. For each item in #4, write down in detail the type of person you need to be to have/get this in your life.

Compassion: a sympathetic pity and concern for the sufferings or misfortunes of other is what motivates people to go out of their way to help the physical, mental, or emotional pains of another and themselves.

Compassion involves allowing ourselves to be moved by suffering and experiencing the motivation to help alleviate and prevent it. It's a known and proven fact that the best leader is the best servant.

Compassion is a fundamental pillar for highly effective leadership, however, it has not always enjoyed the level of importance it deserves.

Compassion literally means 'to suffer together.' Among emotion researchers, it is defined as the feeling that arises when you are confronted with another's suffering and feel motivated to relieve that suffering.

Compassion is not the same as empathy or altruism, though the concepts are related. While empathy refers more generally to our ability to take the perspective of and feel the emotions of another person, compassion is when those feelings and thoughts include the desire to help. Altruism, in turn, is the kind, selfless behaviour often prompted by feelings of compassion, though one can feel compassion without acting on it, and altruism isn't always motivated by compassion.

'Do all the good you can and make as little fuss about it as possible.' – Charles Dickens

While cynics may dismiss compassion as touchy-feely or irrational, scientists have started to map the biological basis of compassion, suggesting its deep evolutionary purpose. This research has shown that when we feel compassion, our heart rate slows down, we secrete the "bonding hormone" oxytocin, and regions of the brain linked to empathy, caregiving, and feelings of pleasure light up, which often results in our wanting to approach and care for other people.

Highly effective leaders have managed a crucial transformation which Bill George, former CEO of Medtronic, defined as shifting from "I to We".

Practicing compassion actually results into shifting the focus from self to others, hence compassion is about going from "I" to "We." If we accept the fact that transitioning from "I" to "We" is possibly the most important process of becoming an authentic leader, those who already practice compassion will know how and appreciate the confound impact on their leadership effectiveness.

Here are some specific steps that you can take to cultivate compassion:

- **Show yourself compassion first:**

Most of us tend to be hard on ourselves. We are our own worst critics. If left unchecked this self-criticism can ruthlessly highlight our imperfections making us feel like we're never good enough. We can tame our inner critic by engaging in a constant practice of self-care where we can attend to our needs. It's only when we love ourselves that we can truly offer compassion to others. Prioritize yourself and nurture your self-confidence.

- **Be fully present and step outside your ego:**

To be fully present with someone you must be willing to step outside of the self-defined parameters of your ego. We have to be tuned into the interconnectedness of all things and refrain from the assumption that we are the center of the universe.

Expand your awareness and move beyond the surface barriers that separate you from everyone else and plug into the oneness of the human collective system. When you find yourself judging another individual, try repeating the Sanskrit affirmation 'Tat Tvam Asi' which translates to 'You are that'. Envision their face and see them through your mind's eye as you repeat this mantra.

- **Be willing to put yourself in others' shoes:**

Accept that the world looks different through the lens of others based on their backgrounds, genetic predispositions and personal experiences. I know that this is especially hard when you disagree with someone and you don't condone their actions, but let your curiosity and openness override your urge to criticize. Be willing to ask questions to get deeper insights into the personal perspective of others instead of belittling their thoughts and opinions. From this benevolent state of mind, you'll be better able to hold them with compassion in your heart and feel sympathetic towards their foibles and personal struggles.

Remember that life is hard, and everyone is doing the best that they can. As Plato once said, 'be kind, for everyone you meet is fighting a hard battle.'

- **Become an active listener:**

It's too bad we aren't all taught active listening from the get-go—turns out the form of listening we usually offer and receive is more passive than it should be. While passive listening allows a person to hear and react on cue, active listening involves a person listening to each word, imagining the driving emotions behind what is being said, and regularly feeding back what is being heard to the person speaking. Active listening encourages us to tune in—and in doing this, we can connect more deeply.

- **Practice compassion meditation:**

It's a known fact that general meditation is beneficial but meditating specifically on compassion helps us to become more empathetic people. Compassion meditation is a form of meditation that asks you to focus your thoughts on wishing well-being for others.

Best ways to practice developing your vision:

- **Develop the Habit To Think and Plan:**

You must take the time everyday to think, plan and set the right priorities to become highly creative, useful and proactive. Over time you will find yourself launching quickly and strongly toward your purpose, vision and goals. This will allow yourself to work gradually, easily and continuously while having a laser type focus on your purpose. The result of advanced planning is the huge amount of productive and high valued tasks achieved each day. You will find yourself spending less time with idle socializing, wasting time and working on low value tasks.

Take the time to write down how your life is like if you could have everything you want. Read it every morning and everynight

- **Develop a Sense of Urgency:**

By developing a sense of urgency you can trigger this state of flow. This urgency is an inner drive and desire to get the job done quickly. This Inner drive is an impatience that motivates you to get going and to keep going.

Creating urgency must be done correctly to be effective, and here are 5 ways to achieve it:

i. **Follow examples:** Do not think of yourself as the authority on leadership, especially when it comes to creating a sense of urgency.
ii. Communicate clearly, effectively, and with consistency.
iii. **Lead by example:** Everyone must be committed daily to performing with a sense of urgency and setting that example for the entire team.
iv. **Address the naysayers:** Change management is a very difficult thing and there will, in almost every instance, be naysayers that are next to or completely impossible to get on-board. While it may be difficult, it's during these times that you must make those hard-hitting decisions.
v. **Provide incentive or reward:** Design a performance tracking system and provide regular progress updates to encourage and motivate your followers to continue driving the initiative with urgency.

Chapter Six

What Is A Charity Foundation?

What's a Charity Foundation?

Charity opens the gates of development for various people, who do not have access to various facilities of life. And such people are poor or backward class inhabitants living a tough life. In India and many other countries of the world, there are a lot of people and children living below the poverty line. Out of these, many are found begging on streets, selling books or other small items on traffic signals or working as masons. This class of people and children usually do not have any financial support. In this regard, it becomes the duty of the Indian citizens to help them in every possible manner.

This section of people and children, generally, live a miserable life that includes various days that goes without food. For this purpose and to help them out, charity foundation devoted for them have been initiating. Their main aim has been to contact people, who are willing to donate a part of their earnings for the betterment of poor people. Though, such people do not have basic amenities of life; still, they do not deserve to live a despondent lifestyle. Their contacts and network enable the poor people to see a ray of hope in the kind of help provided by them.

These foundations organize help camps from time to time, through which these destitute people are provided food items, medications, free treatment, education, clothes and water facility. At times, these camps also organize awareness camps to enable the poor people to know about various social evils and ways to eradicate them from the society. Apart from this, one will also find child foundation that deals with improving the life of deprived children.

In our daily course of life, we find a lot of children working as labours in factories and begging on signals. It is not their destiny, but a helplessness that drags them towards doing such things.

With a little contribution from every responsible citizen, it seems that the picture of the poor people and children will portray happiness and contentment. After all, people that have not seen books or have worn good clothes before will surely feel happy in receiving such things. This will ensure them a better lifestyle and will keep them away from getting into wrong habits like drug addiction, alcohol intake and smoking. Charity foundation work continuously for the benefit of children, poor, adults and old aged ones.

There are various old aged people, who wander on streets and beg for their living. Such organization helps them in providing a shelter through old age homes. This makes it comfortable for the poor old people, who have been left out by their children or families.

Anyone can contact these organizations, either through their websites or locate their offices in newspapers and television ads. Helping someone is the best thing one can gift to poor children and people that have been living a distorted life. In fact, it is such a gesture that tends to give a new life to someone, who has only been dreaming of it.

Charity Foundations: Good or Bad?

The main problem is that many charities and uninformed people give away their money without wisdom. There is one NGO with an orphanage. They have 62 kids and need money. One fundraiser they approached asked a very important first question; how many staff do you have? Forty-one salaries are paid out each month. This is not a luxury cruise ship! The lack of funds is no surprise and funding was not delivered because it was clear the people running this orphanage cared more about themselves than the kids. Too many charities are really just a business that someone who wants to help the poor finds as a way to make a living for themselves.

Now we find where the problem lies. The tourist donors never look deeper into the organization to find out where their money goes. This is where the lack of wisdom mixed with too much money and good intentions just wastes precious resources.

The other interesting factor about the problem is that many of the hundreds of charity foundations in the area do not communicate with each other. They keep their projects secret as if it is some big corporate espionage.

Funny thing is that is exactly the reality. The foundations are all vying for grants and donations. In order to beat out the others, they have to keep separate and secret, so the other foundations do not steal their projects and take the grant money away from them.

Needless to say, many of these 'charities' use much of the money they receive to pay themselves a good salary instead of doing what should be done, which is put every penny into the people and projects.

Life is not often what it appears. Good intentions quickly turn into bad results if we do not take the time to explore what we are doing deeply enough. The reason this happens is because people give money out of guilt or self-serving satisfaction to make themselves feel they have done something good for poor people which alleviates their guilt of taking advantage of others in their process of accumulating wealth. Then stories like this one come out exposing the waste so people who would give donations become reluctant and the sincere groups do not get the funds they need.

Rather, if people would do for the sake of doing, help because help is needed rather than help to ease their own feelings of guilt for the comforts and blessings they have (odd as that sounds it is often true), then they would take the time to research where the money is going, put in the effort to make sure that their money is spent wisely, and continue to be active and involved rather than give their tithe at church on Sunday, then go and create a new lot of bad karma with a weekly cleansed slate.

We must know the reason we do what we do, serve the need and not the self. This is the key to success in all endeavours. In Buddhist terms, this is taught as; "Do the best job you can for the sake of doing the best you can." There is no ego involved, rather, there is objective wisdom which leads to the best results rather than looking back in retrospect saying; "It looked like a good idea at the time."

There is a lot that can be done to help people have a better life, and it does not take much money to make a big difference, but rather find the right place to put your money before you hand it over.

Considering Starting Your Own Charity Foundation?

Here is a 10-step guide to starting your own charity:

- **Be the change-maker:**

Identify the exact need or problem you want to address and why. Thoroughly research the need – what's causing the problem, how serious is it and exactly what will solve it? Consider the key questions: what, who, where, when and how? And think about scale: local, national or global?

- **Identify the solution:**

Find a unique solution that will solve the problem you want to address and that, if delivered through a new charity, will be more effective than other attempts – and attract investment.

Find out if charities, institutes, statutory bodies, local groups or global NGOs are already trying to solve this issue. If someone is already in your space, talk to them. Explore the options: could you add value through partnership or support? If your solution seems as simple as providing some personal or company funding, then make sure your funds will make a genuine difference and that setting up a charity is the best financial model. If you can't see anyone addressing the need, then move ahead with your research.

- **Map your 3-10 year journey:**

Include details of your first year of activity. What are you actually going to do and when? What's the big vision, and what small steps will achieve it? Do you want to launch publicly straight away?

- **Plan your fundraising:**

If you need to raise money, where will it come from, how will you raise it, and how much might you need to get off the ground?

Do your research by asking people in similar charities what works for them, or by talking to the Institute of Fundraising. Then decide whether you will ask for donations from individuals, charitable foundations or corporate funders. Find out how much they are likely to give and when. What will you need to invest to raise funds, and who will underpin that investment?

- **Find a friendly and pro bono business finance mentor:**

Look at the big finance picture as well as the detail – the complications of VAT, cash flow and investment. If your expected income is less than £5,000 a year you can set up as an unregistered charity, which gives you more flexibility and less administration and regulation.

As a registered charity you have to provide detailed publicly-available information about your activities, finances, trustees, impact and more. You may also want to set up a company, which then can be registered as a charity – for more help on this, see a lawyer.

- **Think carefully about what your role will be:**

Are you going to be a trustee? In this unpaid role you'll be accountable to the Charity Commission for ensuring the charity's purpose is upheld, and, as a non-executive director to Companies House. Or will you be a paid employee – the chief executive, executive director or manager – responsible to your chair and board? Think carefully about this. Talk to others who have set up charities, both recently and in the past.

- **Seek communications expertise:**

You need to communicate your message effectively to your target audience. This will help significantly in your future fundraising, planning, communications, and engagement of supporters, volunteers and staff. It will also help you think through what you really want to do.

- **Consider your name and brand:**

You need to be visible to future donors, volunteers, partners and beneficiaries, so you'll need a clear and compelling brand. Consider your charity's strapline and descriptors, the "about us" section on your website, your logo, colours, use of media and your Twitter handle – all will be key.

Check out what works best for online search; make sure you know about search analytics, how to position your charity's name as high up the search engine findings as possible. You may want your strapline to tell the story, and the name to be catchy or quirky, or you may want a name that says the obvious.

- **Do you actually need to set up a charity?**

You'll need to fit in with one or more of the 13 charitable purposes, and much more. Check the Charity Commission website thoroughly.

Consider setting up a community interest company or social enterprise instead. Both will enable you to do good with far fewer restrictions. But be aware that quite a few charitable trusts prefer not to donate funds to these types of organisation because they are not perceived to have the purpose and the regulatory safeguards offered by charitable status. You'll need an experienced and supportive lawyer to advise you on these final decisions and processes.

- **Be bold and keep striving:**

It won't always be easy, and you'll certainly face obstacles along the way. But if you're doing something you really believe in – and that makes a genuine difference – the rewards are worth it.

The Distinctions Between Private Foundation and Public Charity

The term "foundation" can be especially confusing, since a non-profit organization can use the term in its name, even it is not an official private foundation.

Difference between public charity and private foundation

What is a Public Charity?

A public charity is a charitable organization that (a) has broad public support, (b) actively functions to support another public charity, or (c) is devoted exclusively to testing for public safety. Many public charities rely on contributions from the general public. Donations to public charities are fully tax deductible to the extent of the law.

Public charities are the organizations people usually think of when they hear the word charity. These non-profits' missions range from helping the poor to easing community tensions to advancing religion, education, or science. Some examples are churches, universities, hospitals, and medical research groups.

A public charity is either "publicly supported" (derives a substantial portion of its support from the public) or functions to "support" one or more organizations that are public charities. More on these supporting organizations here: What is a Supporting Organization?

What is a Private Foundation?

Private foundations are charitable organizations that do not qualify as public charities. In practice, they usually are non-profits that were established with funds from a single source or specific sources, such as family or corporate money – instead of funding from the general public.

Although contributions to private foundations technically are tax deductible, many of these non-profits do not accept donations. Instead, private foundations usually invest their principal funding, then distribute the income from investments for charitable purposes. Many have endowments.

Private foundations generally use these funds to make grants or gifts to other non-profit organizations. In this way, they help charitable, educational, religious, or other causes that help the public.

The IRS recognizes two types of private foundations: private nonoperating foundations and private operating foundations.

Although the IRS uses a number of criteria to distinguish between the two, in practice, the key difference between a private nonoperating foundation and a private operating foundation is how each distributes its income:

- A private nonoperating foundation grants money to other charitable organizations. This is the more common type of private foundation. These foundations do not directly perform any charitable programs or services.
- A private operating foundation distributes funds to its own programs that exist for charitable purposes.

Both types of private foundations are subject to certain restrictions and requirements. For example, they must distribute a specific portion of their income for charitable purposes each year (approximately 5%), they cannot do business with their major contributors, they are subject to excise taxes and can face penalties for self-dealing, making risky investments, and for failing to distribute adequate funds to charitable endeavours, among other regulations.

Every U.S. and foreign charity that qualifies under Section 501(c)(3) of the Internal Revenue Service Code as tax-exempt is considered a private foundation unless it demonstrates to the IRS that it falls into another category. Broadly speaking, organizations that are not "private foundations" are considered "public charities."

Major Examples of Private Foundations and Philanthrophy

Warren Buffett made headlines when he gave most of his fortune away to The Bill and Melinda Gates Foundation. His gift sparked conversations and became the number one story around the world.

Here are 5 choices Warren Buffett made to change the marketplace and the world.

- **Warren Buffett chose to build lives, not family dynasties:**

Warren Buffett called inherited wealth, "food stamps for the rich." He also said not to give your children too little that they can't do anything. Don't give them too much that they do nothing.

Warren Buffett did give his children a substantial amount, but nothing near the 30 billion that The Bill and Melinda Gates Foundation received. His focus was on the potential impact his gift could make to transform lives.

You, too, are responsible for leaving an inheritance to your children and "your children's children." However, you should also focus on ways to impact others beyond your intimate circle. How are you using your skills or tools in the marketplace to transform lives with the time and resources you have been given?

- **Warren Buffett chose to lift up others and remain in the background:**

After giving away 30 billion dollars, Buffett did not ask the Gates to have a foundation named after him. Instead, he chose to have his investment speak through the lives of those who would benefit from his gift.

Let others speak well of you in the marketplace. A good name is to be chosen above riches. What are others 'testifying' about you in the marketplace?

- **Warren Buffett chose to give more to someone who had much:**

Bill Gates did not 'need' the money. In the late 1990's, Bill Gates stated that he expected to retire around 2007 to focus on how to give his money away. Warren Buffett remarked at that time, "He (Bill Gates) will spend time at some point thinking about the impact his philanthropy can have. He is too imaginative to just do conventional gifts."

In the parable of the talents, one additional talent was given to the servant who had five talents because he knew how to increase what he had been given to benefit others.

When you reach the place of acquiring the goals you set for yourself, will you forget your responsibility to others? Will you sow into the lives of others as an ambassador of goodwill? Will your possessions possess you or will you possess them to transform your world?

Do you have to wait until someday? What can you do today with what you have been given? Your contribution is based on your ability, not the quantity.

- **Warren Buffett chose to leave a living legacy:**

Warren Buffett has the pleasure of seeing how his wealth can benefit more lives than he ever thought possible by partnering with someone with vision, the commitment and track record to carry it out.

Who are your partners in the marketplace? How can you work together so that others see what is possible for their lives by looking at you?

- **Warren Buffett chose to believe that when he gave abundantly, he still had more than enough to live out his days wealthy and joyfully:**

Warren Buffett counted the cost and gave joyfully. It is reported that his goal is to give away 85% of his estimated 80 billion dollar wealth. Those who give generously will always have more to give in the future.

The billionaire has pledged to give away the vast majority of his fortune over his lifetime and on his death and has already donated roughly $34bn since 2006. His most recent donations will go to institutions including the Bill & Melinda Gates Foundation, the Susan Thompson Buffett Foundation and the Sherwood Foundation.

The Creator continuously gives seed to the sower. What you produce provides for the needs of the receiver, a continuous supply to you, the giver and gives honor to the Source of all blessings.

Warren Buffett got the world's attention by doing an unconventional thing in the marketplace-giving the bulk of his wealth away joyfully.

What unconventional thing are you doing to get 'your world's' attention? The marketplace is ready to receive the gift that only you can give.

Public Charities That Act as Foundations

A number of non-profits that grant money to public charities are actually public charities themselves. Community foundations and the United Way are examples of such organizations. Many of these non-profits accept tax-deductible contributions to fund their grant making programs.

The early stages of launching a 501(c)(3) non-profit can be overwhelming for the first-time non-profit founder. Once you have figured out your cause, your programs, and have some plan for sustainability, the real work begins. The IRS application for exemption (Form 1023) is long and tedious, and the explanations for what it all means are not always clear. The first issue that can trip up those filling out the application is the distinction between a private foundation and public charity.

The IRS categorizes 501(c)(3) organizations as either private foundations or public charities. By far, the preferred status for most non-profits is public charity status. Private foundation status is the default, unless your organization fits into the exceptions that provide public charity status. The advantages of public charity status are many and varied, and it is essential to understand the distinction between the classifications and how to fit into public charity (when there is a choice).

Private foundations are subject to far more regulation than public charities and are restricted from acts of self-dealing, maintaining excess business holdings, jeopardizing investments, and making certain expenditures. They also must meet minimum distribution requirements. The reporting requirements are burdensome, as well, with a more complex information return that must be filed annually.

Public charities are exempt from taxation on net investment income and certain federal excise taxes, where foundations must pay. Public charities also are in a better fundraising position due to several factors. First, higher dollar limits apply to contributions made by individuals and corporations to public charities, meaning the philanthropic folks interested in your cause benefit more from giving high dollar donations if you are a public charity. Public charities are also the only classification of 501(c)(3) organizations that may also establish and maintain pooled income funds. And, the expenditure rules that foundations are under make it far more likely that public charities can and will receive grant funding from private foundations.

There are four basic types of 501(c)(3) organizations that qualify as public charities. They are:

1. Organizations that engage in inherently public activities: Typically, churches, schools, hospitals, and governmental units meet this criterion.

2. Publicly supported organizations: Organizations that receive a substantial amount of their financial support from the public or government, or through purpose-related activities. This is the most common exception for 501(c)(3) public charities, and the primary test is the 1/3 support test. That is, at least one-third of the organization's total support must qualify as public support.

3. Supporting organizations: Essentially created to allow foundation-like organizations to qualify as charities as long as they are closely tied to an actual publicly-supported non-profit, these organizations suffered from abuse at the hand of controlling interests. Recent changes in the law have tightened the oversight and limitations on these opportunities.

4. Organizations that test for public safety: This provision was added for organizations that test consumer products to determine their acceptability of use by the general public.

In most cases, the best route for public charity status is under the publicly supported organizations exception. Whatever your non-profit idea, planning for a broad base of public support will both allow the highly preferable public charity status and will improve the organization's chances to survive and thrive.

How Does a Charity Work?

Charities in the U.S. exist to fill needs that government cannot address. More than 1.4 million charities hold 501(c)(3) designation from the Internal Revenue Service, according to the National Centre for Charitable Statistics.

This makes them eligible to accept tax-deductible donations and exempt paying federal taxes. A 501(c)(3) organization is either a public charity, private foundation or a private operating foundation. They operate differently but must adhere to IRS regulations to keep their charitable status.

- **Charitable Finances**

Although private foundations and private operating foundations provide financial support to educational, medical and cultural entities and activities, most people associate public charities with the 501(c)(3) designation. Foundations, including the Pittsburgh Foundation, Wal-Mart Foundation and Bill and Melinda Gates Foundation, operate on money raised through earnings on investments and dollars given by one individual, family or business.

Public charities, such as the American Red Cross and United Way get their funding through donations from government agencies, a broad base of individual donors and foundations.

- **Public Charity Leadership**

Public charities, like corporations, have a board of directors to keep them on track with their mission and to monitor their financial health. However, the directors on a non-profit board do not get paid for attending meetings like their corporate counterparts. Small charities with few employees rely on the directors for help with marketing, human resources and accounting; directors for large charities sit on committees for specific functional areas such as compensation, programs and development or fundraising to finance the organization's operations.

Regardless of the size of the charity, the board of directors appoints an executive director to handle day-to-day operations.

- **Private Foundation Structure**

Trustees oversee foundations. They decide what grants the foundation will make, control its investment portfolio and, in small foundations, manage day-to-day affairs. Trustees of large foundations elect officers to fulfil management responsibilities. The board of trustees has to ensure that annual grants total the minimum distribution required by the foundation's articles of incorporation upon which the IRS based its non-profit status. Grants must also fund charitable projects and activities in non-profits such as community agencies, schools and hospitals to meet IRS qualified distribution requirements.

- **Legal Obligations**

Charitable organizations operate under the IRS and public scrutiny. They cannot participate in political campaigns to maintain their tax-free status. When accepting donations, they must provide donors giving a $250 cash gift or property valued at least $75 a written receipt.

Directors and trustees cannot benefit from the charity's activities, a situation known as conflict of interest. For example, a board member cannot use her association with the charity to sell products her company makes.

Public charities must make their tax returns and application for exemption available to the public. Their record keeping must document all monetary distributions and non-financial activities.

Chapter Seven

Who Says Foundations Can't Make Money?

A private foundation is an independent legal entity set up for solely charitable purposes. Unlike a public charity, which relies on public fundraising to support its activities, the funding for a private foundation typically comes from a single individual, a family, or a corporation, which receives a tax deduction for donations.

The word "foundation" is commonly incorporated into the names of many different types of non-profits (e.g., The Susan G. Komen Foundation, The Bill and Melinda Gates Foundation, Make-A-Wish Foundation). But not all of these "charitable foundations" are private foundations. In fact, a private foundation is a very specific and distinct type of charitable foundation.

Both public charities and private foundations are classified as tax-exempt, 501(c)(3) organizations by the IRS. However, the major difference between a private foundation, like The Bill and Melinda Gates Foundation, and a public charity, like the Make-A-Wish Foundation, is where they derive their financial support. While a public charity gets its funding from the general public, a private foundation usually has one source of funding, typically an individual, family, or corporation.

Because a private foundation stays under the control of the donor, you determine:

- The foundation's mission;
- Whom to include on the foundation board;
- Where the funds are invested; and

- How and where funds are given away.

And, because the foundation can be set up with the intent to exist in perpetuity, your charitable giving can continue as long as your foundation exists. In this way, it can become a living family heirloom that's passed from one generation to the next.

Different Types Of Foundations

Many different types of non-profit organizations call themselves a "foundation," or use the word in their names. Here are some examples:

- **Public Foundation:**

A "public foundation" is just another term for a public charity. (Examples of public charities with the word "foundation" in their names include the Make-A-Wish Foundation and The Susan G. Komen Foundation.)

These non-profit organizations rely on donations from individuals, the government, corporations, and private foundations to fund their operations and programs.

- **Private Foundation:**

A private foundation, like a public charity or public foundation, is dedicated to carrying out a charitable mission. However, a private foundation is not a public charity because, instead of receiving public support, it is funded and controlled by an individual, family, or corporation.

Examples of private foundations include The Bill and Melinda Gates Foundation, the Walton Family Foundation, and the Coca-Cola Foundation, Inc.

All private foundations share these commonalities:

- They are established for charitable purposes and to provide donors with a tax deduction for their contributions.
- They are managed by their own board of directors.
- They receive most of their financial support from and are normally controlled by their founders.
- They must make charitable distributions throughout their taxable year.
- They are tax-exempt organizations but must pay a nominal excise tax of 1.39% on their net investment income.
- Although they typically make grants to public charities, they can also:
- Run programs, provide services, and conduct direct charitable activities.
- Provide aid to individuals and families for disaster relief and hardship assistance.

Non-Operating Vs. Operating Foundations

There are two distinct categories of private foundations:

- Non-Operating Foundations
- Operating Foundations

At the most basic level, the primary difference between non-operating foundations and operating foundations is the extent to which a foundation's resources and operations are dedicated directly to charitable activities and services, and whether such operations are carried on continuously or merely sporadically.

- **Non-Operating Foundations:**

These foundations typically make grants to public charities, and they make up the vast majority of the private foundation community. They can conduct their own direct charitable activities (and make grants to individuals, award scholarships, make grants to international organizations that aren't recognized as 501(c)(3) charities, etc.), but running their own programs is not their primary focus.

Generally, a non-operating foundation must make an annual distribution equal to roughly 5% of its prior year's average net investment assets. Distributions that count toward this requirement include grants to charities, certain related expenses, and, with the exception of investment expenses, necessary and reasonable administrative costs (including Foundation Source's annual fee). These foundations are the kind that Foundation Source establishes and supports.

- **Operating Foundations:**

An operating foundation predominantly undertakes charitable activities and must be significantly involved in its own projects in a continuing and sustaining fashion. (Examples might include the operation of a museum, zoo, library, or research facility.) To ensure that operating foundations are adequately engaged in directly carrying out their charitable activities, each year, they are required to spend the major portion of their investment income (85%) directly on the active conduct of their charitable operations (direct charitable expenditures). Essentially, an operating foundation makes direct charitable expenditures by conducting its own charitable projects rather than by making grants to other organizations. (For instance, rather than give a grant to a food bank, an operating foundation might purchase food directly and hire a driver to deliver it.)

Private Foundation Rules

Because private foundations are established for charitable purposes, they must comply with IRS rules to ensure that they are active, and their expenditures benefit the public. A private foundation is therefore required to make an annual distribution equal to roughly 5% of its prior year's average net investment assets. Distributions that count toward this requirement include grants to charities, certain related expenses, and, with the exception of investment expenses, necessary and reasonable administrative costs (including Foundation Source's annual fee).

In exchange for complying with these requirements, private foundation donors enjoy full control over how the foundation's charitable assets are invested and granted (and pass this control to subsequent generations in perpetuity). They are also entitled to significant tax benefits.

A donor may be able to take advantage of three main tax benefits when he or she gives to a private foundation:

- Reduction of the donor's income tax for each year in which a contribution is made;
- Avoidance of capital gains taxes depending on the characteristics of property contributed; and
- Reduction or elimination of potential estate taxes.

- **Income Tax Savings:**

One of the more immediate tax benefits is that a donor will receive an income tax deduction for any amount he or she contributes to a private foundation up to 30% of the donor's adjusted gross income (AGI).

- **Capital Gains Tax Savings:**

In addition to a deduction for income taxes on gifts to a private foundation, donors may also be able to avoid paying capital gains taxes by donating highly appreciated assets to a private foundation. For example, if a donor were to give appreciated stock to a foundation, he or she would be entitled to receive an income tax deduction for the full, fair-market value of the stock. When the foundation decides to sell the stock in the future, it will pay only the nominal excise tax of 1.39% on the net capital gains.

- **Estate Tax Savings**

When assets are contributed to a private foundation, they are excluded from the donor's estate and, as a result, are not subject to either federal or state estate taxes. For high-net-worth individuals who have a strong charitable interest, private foundations offer an opportunity to avoid paying estate taxes while simultaneously creating a lasting philanthropic legacy.

Benefits Of A Private Foundation Vs. A Public Charity

According to the National Center for Charitable Statistics, there are approximately 1,097,689 public charities in the United States, and perhaps just 90,000 private foundations. The reason why public foundations vastly outnumber private foundations is largely explained by financial considerations: A public charity can solicit support from the general public, government, and private foundations whereas a private foundation is funded by an individual, family, or corporation. Although Foundation Source has lowered the cost of starting and managing a private foundation, making it practical to establish a private foundation with as little as $250,000 in initial funding, public charities often have lower start-up costs and no minimal revenue requirements.

Tax Deductible Giving Limits of Public Charities and Private Foundations

Public charities must pass various support tests to qualify for their IRS status. However, compared to private foundations, public charities do have a somewhat higher limit on how much a donor may give and still receive a tax deduction.

A donor may receive up to 60% of his or her adjusted gross income (AGI) for cash donations to a public charity, and up to 30% AGI for donations to a private foundation. In practice, however, tax deduction limitations rarely present a barrier to private foundation donors. First, many donors do not reach AGI limits on tax deductions. If they do, however, contributions that exceed annual limits may be carried over to subsequent years.

Second, contributions may be made both to a private foundation and a public charity, so if the maximum 30% AGI limit of cash contributions to a private foundation is reached, additional cash contributions of up to 30% AGI can be made directly to one or more public charities.

Advantages of Private Foundations over Public Charities

Beyond these differences, private foundations enjoy important advantages over public charities. The most important one of these is control. Unlike public charities, which are governed by diversified boards of directors, private foundations are independent legal entities controlled exclusively by their donors. The donors have the final say on how foundation assets are invested and spent; which charities to support; whether others share in foundation governance; and if so, how.

Moreover, because private foundations are given very broad latitude by the IRS to pursue their missions, they can effect change in many ways beyond granting to public charities. A private foundation is empowered to work through almost any entity, public or private, to accomplish its charitable objectives. In addition to supporting public charities, a private foundation may:

- Make international grants.
- Award scholarships (and choose the recipients).
- Give funds directly to individuals for disaster relief and hardship assistance.
- Make Program-Related Investments including loans, loan guarantees, and even investments in for-profit businesses.
- Run their own charitable programs.

A private foundation provides both control and flexibility, making it an ideal charitable vehicle for donors who want to transform equity into purpose.

Benefits of a Private Foundation:

As charitable entities, private foundations have proven to be incredibly successful engines of positive change. In the 20th century, private foundations helped bring about everything from Sesame Street to the white lines on the highways and the 911 emergency system, and their transformative work continues, powering solutions to environmental challenges, poverty, and other persistent problems.

Although the funds and activities of private foundations serve the public, these charitable vehicles do offer significant benefits for donors as well, enabling them to:

- **Leave A Personal And Family Legacy:**

The majority of foundations are set up to exist in perpetuity. This means that control over the foundation and its assets can be passed to countless generations of family, perpetuating your values, continuing your charitable work, and burnishing your name far beyond your lifetime. Today, Carnegie and Rockefeller are better remembered for their philanthropic legacies than for their accomplishments in the steel and oil industries. And because gifts are made from an endowment that generates investment revenue, the total gifts made by the foundation over time can far surpass the initial funding.

- **Engaging Family In Philanthropy:**

A private foundation provides ample opportunities for teaching children and young adults about giving back while making philanthropy a family affair. Here are five of the most important benefits of a private foundation for families:

They help instil values and traditions: Involving the next generation in your philanthropy is one way to ensure that your family's charitable legacy endures. The process of working together as a family can instil philanthropic values that last a lifetime. Moreover, because private foundations are often established to exist in perpetuity, handed down from one generation to the next, your foundation can produce generation upon generation of individuals who are committed to making a difference.

- **Maintain family ties:**

In our increasingly geographically dispersed society, the family foundation can be the glue that maintains connections as family members move to pursue college and start careers and families across the country or even the globe. Foundation meetings and regular opportunities for collaboration provide a "non-Thanksgiving" reason for the family to get together, talk, and share how they might make a difference.

- **Deepen social consciousness:**

The rapid pace of modern life offers few opportunities for families to work together on significant issues that are meaningful to them. Competing priorities—work, kids' activities, social obligations, exercise, entertainment and travel—make it difficult for families to find time to talk about things that matter, let alone take action on those issues. For many families, the private foundation becomes the "hearth" around which multiple generations gather to discuss problems they would like to see resolved. In the process, family members get to know each other on a whole new level—moving conversations beyond "what did you do today?" to discussing issues truly important to the family.

- **Increase personal fulfilment:**

Giving can make us happier. In a classic exercise, psychologist and researcher Martin Seligman asked his students to engage in one pleasurable activity and one philanthropic activity and then write about both. According to the students' accounts, the perceived aftereffects of the fun activity (watching a film, eating ice cream) paled in comparison to the altruistic venture (volunteering in a soup kitchen). Why was this? The research indicated that the process of giving took the students outside themselves. The total engagement and loss of self-consciousness they experienced when helping others had a stronger and more lasting impact than the short-lived stimulation of the "fun" activity.

- **Develop "real-world" skills:**

Involving the younger generation in the foundation can build practical competencies such as leadership, teamwork, investment management, negotiation, and social awareness. While the family foundation can provide young adults with significant opportunities for career development, even school-age children can benefit from the opportunity to apply their developing skills.

So what is the right age to start exposing your children to philanthropy? Some clients feel it's a good idea to start as early as possible, opining that life's lessons are taught early across the dinner table. That way, by the time children are old enough to join the foundation, philanthropy has already been an integral part of their lives. Other clients feel it's better to wait because a heavy-handed approach can backfire and lead to resentment or rebellion. They believe that delaying until a young person is ready to take on the responsibility of foundation involvement fosters a genuine desire that comes from a place of maturity. In our view, there is no right choice—each family must make its own decision. Whichever path you choose, engaging the next generation should be an ongoing process that is constantly reinforced, not a one-time event.

- **Receive Tax Deductions & Other Benefits From Charitable Giving:**

Giving through a private foundation offers tremendous advantages over giving as an individual. Not only can you magnify your philanthropic impact, establish your personal legacy, and help bring your family together, but they offer these financial benefits as well:

Tax Savings for You and Your Estate

Giving to a private foundation may make it possible for you to:

- Reduce your income tax for each year in which you make a contribution
- Avoid capital gains taxes depending on the characteristics of property contributed
- Reduce or eliminate potential estate taxes

Grow your charitable funds in a tax-advantaged environment, and pass control of them to future generations to continue your philanthropy.

- **Income Tax Savings:**

One of the more immediate tax benefits is that a donor will receive an income tax deduction for any amount he or she contributes to a private foundation up to 30% of the donor's adjusted gross income (AGI). Although you get the tax deduction up front, you can make your charitable deductions over time, enabling you to give thoughtfully.

- **Capital Gains Tax Savings:**

In addition to a deduction for income taxes on gifts to a private foundation, donors may also be able to avoid paying capital gains taxes by donating highly appreciated assets to a private foundation. For example, if a donor were to give appreciated stock to a foundation, he or she would be entitled to receive an income tax deduction for the full, fair-market value of the stock. When the foundation decides to sell the stock in the future, it will pay only the nominal excise tax of 1.39% on the net capital gains.

- **Estate Tax Savings:**

When assets are contributed to a private foundation, they are excluded from the donor's estate and, as a result, are not subject to either federal or state estate taxes. For high-net-worth individuals who have a strong charitable interest, private foundations offer an opportunity to avoid paying estate taxes while simultaneously creating a lasting philanthropic legacy.

- **Tax-Advantaged Growth:**

Because assets you contribute to a private foundation will be able to grow in a tax-advantaged environment, over the years, the foundation's value will likely exceed the total amount of your contributions—despite making regular charitable grants. The result will be a significant charitable legacy that your heirs may continue to control and pass down to future generations in perpetuity.

Tax Benefits Of A Private Foundation

In addition to the many philanthropic and charitable reasons a donor might have for establishing and funding a private foundation, there are also short-term and long-term tax benefits to consider:

Pay Expenses and Hire Staff:

Private foundations have latitude denied to other types of charitable vehicles. For example, they can pay charitable expenses and hire staff—even family members.

- **Pay Expenses:**

When you have a private foundation, all legitimate and reasonable expenses incurred in carrying out your philanthropy count toward your foundation's minimum distribution requirement (the IRS requires that private foundations distribute at least 5% of average investment assets annually). Travel expenses for site visits, board meetings, conferences, office supplies, and even our fees at Foundation Source qualify.

- **Hire Staff:**

Federal tax law permits foundations to pay "reasonable compensation" to qualified staff—even if the foundation is staffed by your family. Foundation Source's optional Compensational Benchmarking Program is available to clients who want to ensure that compliance with IRS regulations.

How does a charity trust/foundation work allow the rich to keep their money?

Charities in the US incorporate as 501c3 corporations. C-level executives of charities typically make less money than executives at for-profits. So, let's say you worked for 20 years and made $20,000,000,000. Now, you're retired. Your annual expenses, including taxes and all other bills amount to, say, $2,000,000. You're paying zero income tax because you are not earning, anymore. You're just living off your $20,000,000,000. You've already fully-paid off your $50,000,000 home and your $10,000,000 car collection and so on. This is all done. You're getting a generous pension. But now what? How do you invest your money so that you make money?

One way of doing it is to start a non-profit. Let's say your non-profit distributes clothes to the needy. And let's say that you're someone like Tommy Hilfiger or Calvin Klein. So you know a little bit about clothing. You put $100,000,000 into your foundation to start the company. Remember, you aren't paying tax on this. You recruit employees and volunteers to go and donate the clothing. So you lose money, say, the first 5 years. Let's say you lose $20,000,000 over 5 years. No problem. You still have $80,000,000. But now, you have the world's attention. People are going to start donating money, clothing, services, etc. Over the next 5 years, you make back the $20,000,000 you lost. And after that, you make more and more money each year.

You get a small salary. You do pay some tax on that. But then, as a C-level executive, you get the company to pay for your travel, your home insurance, your car insurance, etc. Essentially, your costs drop to zero. The company doesn't pay tax because all of these things are expenses and companies only pay tax on what remains after expenses. Besides, the company is getting stuff for free, anyway. In the meanwhile, your company's net worth grows. Gradually, you pull out your original $100,000,000. And that is still tax-free. In fact, the non-profit pays you interest on it because it was a loan. Plus, you got to write off losses of $20,000,000 over the first 5 years, at least.

Now, you tell your clothing company (the one from which you retired) to do business with the non-profit. You are no longer working with either your original company or with your non-profit. Every time the non-profit buys clothes from your company, you get a piece of the profit at both ends because you made the deal happen. And, when you make enough money that way, you start a new non-profit foundation.

Chapter Eight

What do you want to leave behind if you leave the world?

"I've learned that people will forget what you said, people will forget what you did, but people will never forget how you made them feel." —Maya Angelou.

Have you ever asked yourself what your ultimate purpose is; what you are supposed to add to this world and what imprint you will leave on it? Are you living the legacy you hope to leave behind? What will people say about you when you are gone? What is your legacy?

Mark Twain said that people will miss you so much that even the undertaker will feel sad. What kind of mark will you leave on the world? Will it be a better place because you were born? Will the world have more compassion, more love, and more hope because you lived your life with high ideals? Do you put the needs of others first? Do you look for ways to serve and to help?

Author Ray Bradbury wrote in his book Fahrenheit 451, "Everyone must leave something behind when he dies. Something your hand touched some way, so your soul has somewhere to go when you die. It doesn't matter what you do, so long as you change something from the way it was before you touched it into something that's like you after you take your hands away."

Each of us will leave a legacy behind after we pass on; that is a given. It doesn't matter how young or old we are; we never know when our days are up. Would you be proud of the legacy you left behind if your life ended today?

We should each aspire to live our lives every day in ways that cast a positive light on us. Furthermore our lives should set an example that others who follow after us will benefit from.

In essence, living a legacy requires consideration for tomorrow. That does not mean living for the future. To focus on our legacies we must certainly consider future outcomes. But living our legacies means making each moment count, living each moment with intention.

An intention is a course of action, physical, mental, emotional, or spiritual, that one intends to follow. It is an objective or vision that guides our thoughts, attitudes, and choices. We send our intentions out in the form of a thought, but we must fulfil their destination with our deliberate actions. This is important because you are building your legacy every day, whether by intention or not.

A life that just happens does not inspire anyone. No one will remember it. So the most important question to ask ourselves when planning our legacy is, "In what light do I want to be remembered. Will others see my life as having been lived to the fullest, or will they see it as a life of someone who just got by?"

Ultimately, we have no control over how others will remember us, but we certainly can influence it. To do that we must have a direction-we must identify what we want to contribute and achieve while we are here.

Whatever we achieve in life, the knowledge we acquire, and the challenges we rise above, gets passed down through the generations that follow after us. Our words and actions become ripples in the sea of time. They will impact the lives of our family, friends, and community, and continue to carry on long after we are gone. The legacy of our lives will impact the lives of those we hold dearest-our children, grandchildren, great-grandchildren, and future generations. Our words and actions of today influence the way we will be remembered tomorrow. What stories and memories will you leave behind?

Everyone will be remembered for something. We all hope to be remembered in a positive light. That memory is influenced by the way we live our day-to-day life, by our attitudes, outlooks, values, and convictions. It is better to be remembered as an optimistic person than a pessimistic person. It is better to be remembered for our inner strength than for our weakness. It is better to be remembered as a faithful person than one who is faithless. And it is better to be remembered as one who is kind than one who is hostile.

Are you living a life of intention or do you merely exist? Are you living the life that is best suited for you and your uniqueness or are you living the life that others want you to live? Are you following your heart or following the crowd?

Hope to leave a legacy of love?

If so, there are many ways for you to do that. You can be a loyal, true person who supports and celebrates the successes of others. You can treat others with compassion, and kindness. You can love deeply and unconditionally. You can teach others to fight for what they believe in. You can advocate for those who cannot advocate for themselves. You can be charitable.

You can be accepting and forgiving. You can nurture and respect all creation; the Earth, animals, and the family of mankind. You can love life. You can spread light. You can love yourself. And you can allow others to love you.

Hope to leave a legacy of purpose?

Leaving a legacy of purpose requires living for purposes greater than our selves. To live for purpose we must positively impact the world while we are here as well as long after we are gone. We can do that through the generosity of our time and service or through financial endowments. Some people donate money while they are alive.

Some bequest their estates to charities, religious institutions, or scholarship funds after they pass on. But one does not have to have money to leave a legacy of purpose. For most people it is the work they do in life that leaves a legacy of purpose, whether for individuals, a business, a foundation, a non-profit organization, school, or religious institutions.

Legacy of excellence or inspiration?

You can accomplish this by pursuing excellence in something or everything to inspire excellence in those around you. You can encourage others to raise the bar on their own standards. Strive to make a difference in whatever situation you are committed to whether through outstanding teaching, school, charitable work, parenting, the arts, or the business world. Inspire and teach others to have hope, whether through your words or messages, or by quiet example.

Call on the adversity you have risen above or the difficult feats you have bravely achieved to accomplish wonderful things with your life. Your diligence and optimistic outlook is what helped you reach and exceed your goals. Others are empowered by your exemplary life, and the legacy continues.

Legacy of encouragement?

Be someone who encourages and stands behind others cheering them on. Know how to treat people with respect. Make others feel special. Be generous with praise and gentle with criticism. Lend a helpful hand to those who are giving their best effort but may still be struggling.

Be considerate of the well-being of others. Offer help to those who are striving to reach their goals. Parents, spouses, friends, teachers, and co-workers have the greatest opportunities to leave legacies of encouragement.

Leaving a legacy does not require financial wealth or notoriety. There are many unsung heroes walking or who have walked this Earth. Each of us plays an essential part in the overall puzzle of life. All our lives have meaning, influence, and purpose. Each of us has something remarkable to pass on to our descendants and to the world.

Living your life with a positive attitude, hopeful outlook, honourable value system, and clear conviction will create a legacy that others will remember long after you are gone. A life lived virtuously and consciously ripples and reverberates eternal. That is the legacy of unsung heroes.

That is one of the legacies I hope to leave behind and try to live every aspect of my life with that goal in mind. There is a part of me, the ego part I suppose that wants to see the difference I am making. I also know that there is so much I cannot see that profoundly affects my life, the lives of others, the universe, and the spiritual world. I don't necessarily have to see the total impact my life is making to know that I am making one.

Those of us who have children will certainly leave a legacy for them. If we love our children, the legacy we leave should be a positive one.

My goal in raising my children was to break the dysfunctional patterns of my heritage, the problematic legacy that had been left for me. It took most of my life to break the debilitating cycle I inherited but through tenacity I succeeded. I got professional help for myself and made conscious choices in raising my children. I refused to subject them to a life of emotional uphill climbing; to emotionally saddle them with the problems of my past.

They have been fortunate to not have to back-pedal through life as I did. They are both living wonderful, successful, progressive, and happy lives. They are making healthy choices. That is the legacy I will leave them and the generations that come after them. If I accomplish nothing else in life, I will leave this Earth fulfilled.

Everyone has a different perspective so not everyone will see things from my point of view. My perspective works for me and I hope to inspire others with it. But there are many ways that we can impact the future and leave our mark on it, many ways we can leave a legacy that will stand the test of time.

Step outside of yourself for a minute and view yourself from the outside looking in. How do others see you? Evaluate your morals, values, and beliefs. Would you be proud for others to follow in your footsteps? Assess what areas you can improve on and then take action immediately.

As long as you live and breathe you can change what is not working in your life. The problem is we never know when we will stop living and breathing. That is why we should never hesitate to make positive changes as soon as we realize they need to be made.

A legacy is a reflection of your uniqueness and self-expression. What personality traits or innate gifts do you possess that seem to have the most impact on others? Is it your morals and character, your generous heart, your ability to inspire others, or your peaceful nature? Is it your talents, your sense of humour, your idiosyncrasies, or your intellect?

Now think about the interests and issues that arouse your enthusiasm. Do you want to make a difference in causes such as child abuse, animal abuse, homelessness, health issues, or better education for our children? Are you civic-minded and strive for changes in your community or country? Are you passionate about making global changes such as world peace, saving the environment, world hunger, or stopping the spread of disease?

Next think about the largess of your impact. Do you want to leave a legacy for your children and grandchildren? Will you be happy with a legacy that stays within the family tree for generations to come? Would you like to make a difference in someone's life through vehicles such as adoption, foster care, or volunteering? Do you want to impact the survivors of a cause? Are you hoping to be famous? Do you want to leave your indelible mark on mankind?

Once you have narrowed down the area or areas you would like to focus on you may need a plan to help you implement it. Your plan should include short-term and long-term strategies. Be flexible and understand that you cannot achieve everything at once. Life is a series of processes. Life is continuously unfolding.

Everything shifts and changes over time. Your reality today may not be your reality tomorrow, next month, or next year.

Evaluate where you are now in your life and then think about the direction you want your legacy to take you. How will you implement moving towards your goal? Perhaps you have gifts that you have not shared with others and would like to; assets you believe others would benefit from. Maybe you have regrets about something you have done to someone in the past and have not yet made amends for but hope to. Maybe you have been longing to document your life in a journal or write a book.

Planning the legacy you want to leave for the generations who follow after you is a loving act. None of us will live forever but we should all leave behind a positive part of us that will.

How are you living your life currently? Start planning the direction you want your legacy to take you and begin moving towards your goal.

We don't have to be a rock star or a president to leave a legacy. A legacy is like a drop of water. The drop never reaches the shore, but the ripples it creates will extend outward to the shore.

Our impact on the world will likely be greater than we imagine it today, but there are some things we might start doing now that can insure the tomorrows of our legacy.

Here are some things to chew on:

- **Show kindness:**

The greatest legacy is that of kindness, compassion and love towards others. Commit yourself daily to taking part in the lives of those around you and to performing random acts of kindness. This will not only impact your legacy; it will also impact the quality of life you live today. We benefit when others are blessed by our investing in their lives.

- **Maintain a positive attitude:**

Winston Churchill once said, "I am an optimist. It does not seem too much use being anything else." Only a positive attitude can have a positive influence. As we get older, we may have a tendency to be a bit too cynical about nearly everything. However, making a lasting impact requires us to believe that change is possible. Don't let your legacy be a sequel to Grumpy Old Men.

- **Influence change:**

Impact, by its very definition, implies change. Influencing positive change is not a matter of simply performing your best; it is your ability to bring out the best in others. It is this influence that will be remembered by those who carry on your legacy. Mentoring others as opposed to doing yourself should more and more reflect your role in the community and the lives of those around you.

- **Do something meaningful:**

Perhaps a better word is practical. It doesn't have to be anything earth-shattering in order to make a difference. Most communities have numerous organizations that in some way benefit a segment of the community. And they're often short of people who are committed to 'the work.' It could be your church or local youth club. Search yourself, your interests, strengths and experiences. Begin by simply finding out what is going on, talk to people and go to a couple of meetings.

- **Make your vision known:**

Clearly articulating your vision will inspire those who follow you to take up the banner after you are gone. Great legacies are not the result of a single isolated event; they are the summation of your own accomplishments and the accomplishments of those you will influence over time.

Martin Luther King had a dream, but if he had not clearly articulated that dream, it would have died with him. Take the time to clarify your dreams, however modest, and be willing to talk about them so as to be able to pass them on to those who follow you.

- **Every great journey begins with a single step:**

A lasting legacy will influence action long after you're gone. We may lament how we have spent our days to this point. Yet, it's never too late to leave a mark.

Oh, and make sure that laughter is something people remember you by. It will bring smiles to those left behind for years to come.

Conclusion

I've quoted Jeffrey Gitomer who continually says, *"I don't care if you know something, I care how good you are at something"* Kind people realize they are not perfect. Kind and intelligent people always know that there is something to learn so keep their eyes and ears open, all the time.

Kindness is the quality of being friendly, generous, and considerate. I would add compassionate to that, which means to be empathetic and sensitive. We look around the world today and we see so much unkindness. From verbal and physical assault to war and killing.

We see television shows where unkindness serves as entertainment. But, of course, we are all spiritual people, and we are almost always kind. Are we not? Actually, there is much unkindness in religion and spirituality today. Our spiritual development requires that we learn to be kind.

Of course, you might agree, those fundamentalists are unkind to people who don't believe the way do. They say that Jesus died for your sins and you'll go to hell if you don't believe; and that gay people are sinners. True, those belief systems do become excuses for a great deal of unkindness today. Historically Christianity has been unkind -- the inquisition, witch burnings, the Crusades, and mass murder of those who disagreed were certainly unkind.

What did Jesus say about how we treat each other? *"But love your enemies, do good to them, and lend to them without expecting to get anything back. Then your reward will be great, and you will be sons of the Most High, because he is kind to the ungrateful and wicked. Be merciful, just as your Father is merciful."* (Luke 6:35-36)

When you encounter someone who is in pain it's not about you being authentic, or you setting them straight, or about you telling the truth. The real question is, "What does this person need right now?" It's about kindness. Kindness is about joining with another person, connecting.

Often we, in our spiritual development, believe we are to set others straight, to fix their attitudes. This is the same as my fundamentalist friends who want me to convert. They want to fix my belief system. When you believe it is your mission to fix someone, you separate yourself from them. You turn them into an object to be changed, rather than seeing them as a person who is putting out a call for love. Our need to fix others' attitudes is really about changing them so that our world will seem right. In the past I wanted others to be positive so that I would feel okay, and so that my world would seem right. It was a projection of my own issues on them.

We cannot positively influence someone from a place of disconnection. If we think we are better, more spiritual, or that we have the right answer for someone, we disconnect. If we want to truly help someone, we need to be kind. That is, we empathize and we express compassion.

Last week I had the perfect opportunity to practice kindness with a neighbor. My neighbor is upset with the children and parents in the neighborhood because the children have been so noisy. Her other next door neighbor is building a play structure right next to her fence, and she fears it will draw all of the children in the neighborhood. This will mean more noise. She called an attorney and has taken action to prevent this structure from being built.

My neighbor came to me stressed and upset. I listened. She hates her job. My neighbor is a highly intelligent woman with a Ph.d. In her personal life she is responsible for the well-being of another person who is very ill. She comes home in the evening wanting to rest and relax, only to find children yelling and screaming near her house.

People create their own stress. I know this for myself and I teach it. I didn't tell her that. I empathized. And when she referred to some our neighbors as "those people", I stated very clearly that they weren't "those people" to me. They were my neighbors.

My neighbor didn't need a lecture on the causes of stress. She didn't need her attitude adjusted. She needed to be heard and understood. She needed not to be judged, but accepted. She didn't need for me to join her in her drama, or to take her side.

Being spiritual is about unity. It means that you look for ways to join with people, not for ways to separate yourself. The voice of your ego will encourage you to be right, to be special, and to turn others into objects. Next it will justify and defend your behavior. The Voice of Spirit will tell you to listen and to give people what they need. It will tell you to be kind.

Kindness doesn't mean being nice. Niceness can be patronizing or manipulative. Niceness is superficial. Niceness maintains your sense of separation. When we are "nice" to people we expect them to be nice back to us. When we are truly kind we have no expectations. We are kind because that is who we are.

The key to kindness is empathizing with a person's plight, yet seeing through the conditions and acknowledging within your mind the powerful spiritual being who is before you. They don't need a lecture on being positive. They need you to see them as already whole, already well, and already blessed. Your words are acknowledging the conditions, the pain, and how they must feel.

Who you are is acknowledging their spiritual reality. Who you are will come through and have a positive effect.

If you are caught up in someone's condition or in their attitude, it is your issue that needs work, not theirs. Work on releasing your judgments and replacing them with unconditional love and acceptance. Then behave in ways that make sense for the situation.

The practice of kindness is necessary to our spiritual growth. Every person you encounter is an opportunity to practice the spirit of kindness. Don't forget to practice kindness toward yourself. Release your self judgments and guilt and accept yourself where you are now. It feels better to be kind than it does to judge. Practicing kindness will have you feeling lighter, more joyous, and peaceful. Thank God that you are not the manager of the Universe, and that it is not your job to change other people. It is your job to change how you see others, and then to be kind.

Kindness is not a weakness.

Getting someone else told off may feed the ego but it never attracts friends. Arrogance feeds your ego and does not lead to career opportunities. People do not go out of their way to help arrogant people; they go out of their way to help kind people.

Kindness pays, always! In Napoleon Hills book, Think & Grow Rich, he stresses the impact of being kind. He explains that kindness is not becoming a doormat for others. Kindness provides opportunities to add value. One that provides value in a kind way is never a doormat. Arrogant people may try to treat kind people as a doormat but it never works.

I witnessed a client, Barry, going out of his way to help another. Barry did not have the expertise but knew someone that did. "May I virtually introduce the two of you? My contact may have a perspective that may provide you insight and help you think through your problem."

Barry didn't have to offer any help. Barry didn't have the expertise to help directly. Barry was comfortable enough to know that he didn't know something but could add value by facilitating a meeting. Barry was KIND and offered an introduction. It doesn't matter if the other person took the offer. What is remembered is that Barry is kind. This is smart thing to do because kind stories also spread. This one was heard by an executive that mattered.

It takes effort to be kind. Kindness requires that you build your level of self-esteem and become comfortable with what you don't know. It takes dedication to want to continually be kind and add value. Being a kind person is a totally different perspective on life. Kind people look to add value first. Arrogant people want to show off what they know (and do not realize that they are showing what they don't know).

Kind people have a comfort-level or self-confidence to continue moving forward even if they don't know all the answers. They are comfortable not being in total control of any situation because the fear of not knowing everything does not hold them back. Kind people are open to learning by asking themselves "how good am I" at something. Kind people listen for opportunities to add value... not show off their knowledge.

Kind people are noticed by executives because these individuals are so rare. Great leaders notice kind people because kindness is an essential skill for any great leader. Kind people are offered great opportunities to grow that arrogant people are too stupid to see. People flock to kind people. People follow kind people. Kind people become great leaders.

Offer help at every opportunity. Stories of your kindness will travel to the right people.

Be kind... it is an important leadership skill.

End.